1   MOTORCYCLE RIDER BASICS

DEC 08

CH

MOTORCYCLE RIDER BASICS
Buy a Motorcycle, Start Riding and Avoid the Beginner Mistakes

—Frank Gates —

If you are thinking about buying a motorcycle or you just bought one and want to accelerate the learning curve, cash in on my experience. With this book as a guide, you will be enjoying your motorcycle in no time.

I wish I would have had this book six years ago I could have saved a lot of money, time and hassle. I actually rode thousands of miles;

- On the wrong bike
- Not understanding "Go Where You Look"
- "Friction Zone" clueless
- Wearing gear that just was not right

The best beginner rider thing I did was to go through the MSF Basic Rider course. Buying this book would have been the next.

Reno Street Vibrations 2004

3   MOTORCYCLE RIDER BASICS

MOTORCYCLE RIDER BASICS

Buy a Motorcycle, Start Riding and Avoid the Beginner Mistakes

OR

Motorcycle Rider Basic Beginner and Re-Entry Rider Instructions, Tips, Mistakes, Techniques, Personal & Motorcycle Protective, Safety Gear Descriptions, Selection and Resources.

Frank Gates

WordCutter
Sacramento, California

WARNING: Riding a motorcycle is dangerous and can result in serious injury or death. Safety conscious riders drive defensively, always observe traffic laws and avoid possible hazards. I always recommend that every rider obtains proper training and equipment before riding a motorcycle.

Photos and Graphics by Frank Gates and Irina Gates

13-digit ISBN: 978-0-9818519-0-7

Motorcycle Rider Basics: Buy a Motorcycle, Start Riding and Avoid the Beginner Mistakes

Written By: Frank Gates
Published By: WordCutter
                  Sacramento, CA

First Edition, 2008

Published in the United States of America

Dedication

To my wife, the beautiful and sexy Irina, who encouraged and supported me while turning a blind eye on my Saturday chores to give me more time to spend writing this book.

"You don't stop riding because you get old,
You get old because you stop riding."
~Author Unknown

Contents

Figures

Tables

11 MOTORCYCLE RIDER BASICS

About the Author

Frank Gates was born in 1946 in Santa Monica, CA. He is a second time around motorcycle rider and is passionate about riding, averaging 15,000 miles per year, for the last five years. Frank commutes to work everyday on his Harley in the heat, rain and occasionally, the snow.

Frank Gates

Frank rode as a young man for ten years before parking the bike for a forty year hiatus. An engineer by trade, Frank spent these forty years designing telecommunication networks across North America and Australia. Currently, Frank's day job is technical writing in the aeronautics industry. Frank re-entered the world of motorcycles six years ago at the age of fifty five

You can find Frank in Sacramento, CA. with his wife Irina, working at something that involves any kind of writing. If he is not writing, he is probably riding.

Frank welcomes your comments, suggestions and ideas. You can reach him at

www.WordCutter.com

Warning —Disclaimer

This book is designed to provide information on basic motorcycle riding and equipment. It is sold with the understanding that WordCutter and Frank Gates are not engaged in rendering legal, accounting or other professional services. If legal or other expert assistance is required, the services of a competent professional should be sought.

It is not the purpose of this manual to reprint all the information that is otherwise available to authors and/or publishers, but instead to complement, amplify and supplement other texts. You are urged to read all the available material, learn as much as possible about motorcycle riding and equipment and tailor the information to your individual needs. For more information, see the many resources referenced throughout this manual.

Every effort has been made to make this manual as complete and as accurate as possible. However, there may be mistakes, both typographical and in content. Therefore, this text should be used only as a general guide and not as the ultimate source of motorcycle riding and equipment information. Furthermore, this manual contains information on motorcycle riding and equipment that is current only up to the printing date.

The purpose of this manual is to educate and entertain. Frank Gates and WordCutter shall have neither liability nor responsibility to any person or entity with respect to any loss or damage caused, or alleged to have been caused, directly or indirectly, by the information contained in this book.

If you do not wish to be bound by the above, you may return this book to WordCutter for a full refund.

INTRODUCTION

This book is about how to enjoy riding your motorcycle (primarily) and how to save a lot of money getting everything you need to enjoy your ride. This book is based upon my current six years of riding experience.

I have written this book for motorcycle rider beginners. If you have not made the decision on wither or not to ride a motorcycle, reading this book will fill in some blanks that you may be wondering about.

I have sorted the topics in this book to be in a logical learning sequence. By logical sequence I mean that for example, you need to have decided on some sort of riding style (cruiser, touring, sport-bike) before you can choose the appropriate helmet for that riding style.

Also I assume that you are currently riding or about to be riding and you (like all of us) are faced with finding your way through the morass of decisions on what to wear, rider safety, and all of the rest. This book will guide you. What do I need, where do I get it and how much does it cost is the main theme of this book.

Everything in this book is from my personal experience except where noted. I have shared a lot of personal experience so you (hopefully) do not need to reinvent the wheel.

I hope that this book will give you an occasional chuckle and I have written it in a light, easy to understand manner.

No Affiliations

I am not affiliated with any manufacturer or vendor. I have not given anyone or any particular product any special recognition unless I think that product or person deserves it. If I did not mention some vendor, it does not mean anything other than I did not mention them. I wrote this book simply because I have lived it and I thought that others may benefit from my mistakes and experience. Of course, if I can make some grocery money in the process by selling this book, that would be a good thing.

Feedback

I welcome your comments, criticisms, fresh looks, new information and I really value your stories. If you want to tell me that I screwed up something, please do. If you want to tell me off, be rude or just be plain stupid, keep it to yourself. Life is too short. I try to answer every email or snail mail I receive. I do look forward to hearing from you.

Bottom Line

I have organized this book to make it as easy as possible for you to get what you want out of the book. If you are like me (a detailed orientated engineer) all of the stuff is good in here. Too much information is not enough information, tell me everything!

What Does It Cost

I have included, wherever applicable, a cost table. These costs are typical retail costs to give you a starting point. Shop around and you are likely to find better deals. You will see a lot of this stuff on e-Bay and as you already know, buyer beware.

Resources

I have included a section on resources wherever applicable. I think that no matter how much information I put into this book, there will be a desire for more. The resources section will point you in the right direction. Remember though, with all of the ongoing changes in the world, the links may be obsolete (or you may be redirected) by the time you try them.

What Do I Know?

Riding in the 60's: Kick Start and Push

My Dad and I -- 1946

I started riding about five years ago after a forty year layoff. I have always loved motorcycles and I rode a lot growing up in Los Angeles in the sixties. I didn't know the difference between a dirt bike and a street bike. To me, street and dirt was virtually the same thing. You rode where you wanted, when you wanted. I started up again when I turned fifty five I have ridded about 75,000 miles during the last six years, mostly commuting to work. I consider myself to be an average rider with average riding skills.

I took my first ride and got my first ticket all at the same time while riding a Royal Enfield when I was 14 years old. My dad had brought this Royal Enfield home in a box and it took me what seemed like months to put it together and get it to start. I was so excited about actually hearing it run that I jumped on and blasted out of the garage, around the block, through the corner Stop sign and almost ran over a motorcycle cop who happened to be passing by. I got a ticket and big trouble at home.

Funny thing about motorcycles, I will never forget the thrill of that ride. As short as it was (probably under three minutes) it started a motorcycle fever that is still burning today.

Back then, I had a very different outlook on safety than I do now. I was riding in Levis, a T-shirt and tennis shoes. I didn't even own a helmet and never thought about buying a helmet. In and out of city traffic during rush hour, on sidewalks if handy, cutting through corner gas stations and never looking back. I was the kid that made middle aged drivers shake their heads and start griping about teenagers.

Six Years Ago I Started Riding Again

Forty years later, I decided that it was time to get back on a motorcycle. I talked to Irina, my wife, and she said yes, so I was in business. (In my home, I have a saying, "If momma is happy, everybody is happy.")

I bought a new 2003 HD Sportster 1200, a genuine, all American, rumbling, shaking, Harley Davidson and I became a motorcycle rider.

Wow, a lot had changed in those last forty years. My own sense of immortality was significantly higher and motorcycle technology was light years ahead of my last experience. Traffic was more congested and moved a lot faster than I remembered. About all my earlier experience offered was that I was able to get on the motorcycle and start riding without being taught how to go. Everything else was a culture shock.

Figure 1 Sportster

I was amazed at the cost of a new motorcycle. I paid $12,000 for the new Sportster and all I could think of as I wrote out the check was that I had bought my first house in 1972 for $21,000.

My next surprise was outfitting myself and my wife to ride this shinny new Harley. Two full face helmets, two leather jackets, gloves, chaps and glasses and the Harley dealer had another $1,500 of my hard earned cash. And this was just the basic stuff. There was more.

It was summer and the helmets were so hot we were both (my wife and I) sweating like stuck pigs, so off to the dealer and bought a couple of half helmets and a couple of summer riding jackets. Another $600 goes into the kitty. And that still wasn't the end of it.

And that is one key thing you will get out of this book, how to avoid making all of the mistakes that I made when I was gearing up to go riding.

Re-Entry Rider

Now, let's go back to those teenage rides for a minute. No helmet, tee shirts and riding in and out of traffic (did I mention my nifty, thrifty Honda Fifty?) like I was invincible.

Close calls, hell, I didn't even know what a close call was much less worry about it. Sidewalks, wrong way, flat tires (what was tire pressure?) I was a Tasmanian Devil cut loose on the streets of Los Angeles. Jump on it, screw it on, and go like hell! That was my sophisticated riding style.

Figure 2 Honda 50

Youth is invincible.

Now, today, with years of life experience under my belt, I do know what a close call is and I do notice it. I do worry about it, I must confess that sometimes those bodily functions just take over and I feel like I am watching myself like watching a TV show. Whew! A real pucker experience!

So how do I enjoy the ride without killing myself and worrying myself to death in the process? Well, those years of life experience have taught me that flexibility and compromise is the survival book of life.

When a person in their fifties decides to start riding a motorcycle, it is sort of like the same person deciding to start smoking. Everyone knows that smoking is bad for your health and everyone knows that riding a motorcycle is dangerous. But so is driving a car, SCUBA diving, playing baseball, riding horses and so on. There is an element of risk in just about everything and I have not even mentioned marriage yet.

To me, I weight the fun factor against the risk factor. I say fun factor but it could be the satisfaction factor or the enjoyment factor. Take smoking for example, if the odds are that one out of ten people who smoke are going to die earlier than the other nine, why start smoking in the first place. As a non-smoker, I just do not really see any fun factor and it is a pretty easy decision to stay away from cigarettes.

Motorcycles on the other hand have a different twist. If the odds are that one out of one hundred thousand motorcycle riders are going to die because of riding a motorcycle, well, that is a pretty big number to hide in. Is that the right number, I have no idea and quite honestly, I do not want to get strung out on statistics here. Riding a motorcycle is dangerous, I know it and you know it so enough said! What about the attraction or the fun factor.

There is a mystic about motorcycles that cannot be denied. Even the most distant observer must admit that a motorcycle brings out some sort of emotion in them. It is sort of like flying in a small airplane, no matter how detached you are emotionally from the vehicle (the airplane), you are going to get some feelings bubbling to the surface when you are in one, near one, hear one or just see one crawling across the distant sky.

I think the same holds true for a motorcycle. Just imagining yourself speeding across the ground at 50 miles per hour with nothing between you and that ground but a motor and two wheels is an exhilarating feeling. There exists the flat out thrill of riding the "machine". I think most people have this feeling that's why most people are afraid of riding a motorcycle. It's unnatural; it's crazy, if a man was meant to fly, blah, blah, blah!

Even those who do ride are afraid but with a different kind of fear. Their fear is more of a healthy respect, they are in awe. Of course there are a few crazies that just ride the snot out of a bike without ever thinking about anything at all except just riding the snot out of the bike!

Did I say crazy? Did I say a few? Maybe they are just enthusiasts, maybe there are more than just a few, eh?

On a more grounded and practical level, riding a motorcycle just looks like fun, pure and simple. When you ask motorcycle riders if they like riding, they will almost always give you a big affirmative.

On top of looking like fun, motorcycles are great to get around on, easy to park almost anywhere, great gas mileage, and very, very sexy.

Sexy? Yeah, you do have to admit it that there is something very sexy, very romantic, and very exotic about riding a motorcycle.

I know that it is dangerous and I know that it is fun. What I had to ask myself was how much danger I willing to accept for the promise of how much fun? And for me personally, at this point in my life, the deal looks like a pretty good tradeoff. My decision has been made, put me in coach, I am ready to play.

If you are not ready to play, you really should stay out of the playground. I am not saying that maliciously but compassionately. If you are not mentally, spiritually and physically ready to ride a motorcycle, stay away until you are ready. Being hesitant, nervous and timid will not enhance your motorcycle riding experience.

How do you know if you are ready?

Well, as soon as you find yourself sitting on a motorcycle, engine running, clutch engaged, I'd say you have arrived. Still have a lot of doubts? Good, that's a healthy thing. You will gain experience and minimize the doubts.

I was talking to one of the owners of a Harley shop in California and he told me that he gets a lot of people who come in and plunk down $25,000 for a new Harley. They buy a helmet and fire up the motorcycle and ride off into the sunset. He kind of chuckled about firing up the motorcycle. He said that a lot of these folks were totally clueless about motorcycles, they didn't know the clutch from the brake but with three minutes of instruction, they were off and running. (I guess those folks won't be buying a copy of this book.)

Bottom Line

Riding a motorcycle is dangerous. Riding a motorcycle is fun. Some people ride and some people do not ride. It is an individual choice.

Too Old To Ride, Who Says So?

Three years ago, I was leaving the local Harley shop (Rocklin Harley) here in California. I stopped to admire an unusual Harley. I think it was a Royal Glide or Electra Glide, a big bagger with all of the goodies. It was all white and pink, the bike, the seat and the saddlebags, all white and pink. Interesting, not my style, but someone had put a lot of effort (money) into setting it up this way. It was in a customer parking spot.

I finished being nosey and was getting on my Wide Glide when I noticed a woman walking out of the shop and over to the white and pink Harley. She had on white and pink leathers, the whole shooteroo, jacket, chaps, boots, gloves and helmet, all white and pink. She sat down on the matching bike, put on her helmet, fired the bike up, and walked the bike backwards out of the parking spot. Obviously very experienced, she put it in gear and roared out of the parking lot and down the highway.

What impressed me was not so much the designer coordinated ensemble (she did look very cool) but the fact that she was pretty darn old. I would guess her age at 60 to 70 years old. That impressed me a lot.

So how old is too old to ride?

Hmm, I hear this all of the time. Is it fact or fiction? There are two ways to look at it.

One way to look at it is from the government's perspective. The government has a "too old to ride" filter in place called the drivers license motorcycle endorsement. You need to get this endorsement to ride legally. It makes sense to get the endorsement even just for your own self-confidence. No endorsement, no riding the motorcycle. A simple riding test to make sure you can ride and a simple written test to make sure you understand the laws pertaining to motorcycle operation on the road.

If you fail, does it mean you are too old? No, it means you failed the test. You may actually be too old, maybe you can't actually control the bike, maybe you didn't learn the laws or maybe, you are just too goofy to get the endorsement. Whatever the reason may be, the government's driver's license machine has taken you off the motorcycle and out of the game.

Another way to look at it is from you own perspective. To me that means using plain old common sense.

Physical strength is a consideration.

While you do not need to be Arnold to ride a motorcycle, you do need to have the physical strength necessary to safely ride. Manipulating a 700 pound machine in and out of parking, picking up a downed motorcycle, hard braking, high speed maneuvers, passenger control, it all calls for physical strength.

Experienced riders (like the white and pink lady at the beginning of this chapter) use their experience to leverage their strength. For example, an experienced rider will not intentionally park on a downhill slope which will require manually walking the motorcycle backwards, uphill, against the slope. They will either initially back it into the parking spot or find another place to park.

Tips

- Experienced riders know how to pick up a downed bike using their back strength and the ability to "roll" the bike upright.

We have all seen 100 lb female riders on 700 lb Harley's doing just fine. Just like we have all seen (well at least I have) 300 lb men wrestling their Harley to the ground while trying to walk it around a parking pole. Each individual must make the call on their own physical strength.

Old Bones

Medically, as we grow older, our bones become easier to break and take longer to heal. Our brains rattle around inside our skulls a lot harder when our helmet takes a hard hit than younger brains would rattle around in younger skulls on the same hit. What it all means is that the older motorcycle rider will break easier, with more damage and take longer to heal than the younger motorcycle rider.

Slower Reflexes

This is the next big item. I think that slower reflexes are the trigger for making a decision to stop riding the motorcycle. When you are faced with a 70 mph decision, you do not have the luxury of time. You make your decision and go right now. If you choose wrong, you probably are in trouble but at least you had a choice and at least you made the decision.

If your reflexes hamper your ability to make a timely decision, you probably should not be out riding a motorcycle. Either you are too slow thinking about making a decision or too slow executing the decision once it has been made. Maybe it's a little of both, but ether way, it is time to hang up your chaps. Is this an age thing, a psychological thing? Who cares, the end result is the same.

Strength, reflexes and risk all determine when you are too old to ride. If you do not have what it takes, you can either get what you are missing or get off the bike.

What compounds the decision to stop riding is the same thing that impacts car drivers who need to give up their driver's license. No one wants to stop driving. No car means no freedom and that sucks.

The aging driver's reflexes have slowed down over a period of time (years) and the aging driver feels like everything is OK, just like normal. They just did not notice the change over the years. More often than not, an accident triggers action from the government or loved ones force the driver into mandated driving retirement.

On a motorcycle, the same thing goes on except with the slow reflexes but the results of a minor accident are significantly different. What may be a fender-bender to a car, can be a life threatening crash to motorcyclists. Unlike the car driver, the aging motorcyclists must spot the reflex problem much earlier and decide get off the motorcycle early on.

Tips

- Pay attention to those around you. If they start asking you if you are "Doing OK?", or maybe "Tired yet?" they may be seeing something you are missing. It's kind of like telling a co-worker that they have BO. It's not an easy conversation. Only the ones that love you will tell you the truth. Pay attention.

Bottom Line

I figure that if you are successfully riding a motorcycle, you have enough maturity and common sense to make your own decision on riding. You monitor your own reactions, your close calls, and your overall bike psychic and then, you make the call.

How to Stretch Your $4 Gallon of Gas

OK, my car gets 22 mpg on an average, that's not too bad. It's around 18 mpg in the city and 28 mpg on the highway. I commute 40 miles roundtrip 5 days a week to work, or 200 miles per week. At $4.00 per gallon for gas, it cost me

$$200 \text{ miles}/22 \text{ mpg} = 9.09 \text{ gals per week}$$
$$\$4.00 \text{ per gal} \times 9.09 \text{ gals} = \$36.36 \text{ gas cost per week}$$

My motorcycle (HD FXDWG Wide Glide) gets 44 mpg or twice the mileage of my car. It is twice as efficient as my car when it comes to gas consumption. So using the same commute to work mileage,

$$200 \text{ miles}/44 \text{ mpg} = 4.55 \text{ gals per week}$$
$$\$4.00 \text{ per gal} \times 4.55 \text{ gals} = \$18.18 \text{ gas cost per week}$$
$$\text{Or } 50\% \text{ of the gas cost using my car}$$

Monthly;
Car cost $36.36 per week X 4 weeks = $145.45 per mo.
MC cost $18.18 per week X 4 weeks = $72.72 per mo.

Annualized;
Car cost $145.45 per mo. X 12 mo. = $1725.46 per yr.
MC cost $72.72 per mo. X 12 mo. = $872.73 per yr.

This is a savings of $873 per year by using the motorcycle.

Your cost variables are different from mine;
- My daily commute is 50% street and 50% highway, if yours is 100% highway, your gas mileage will

increase approximately 20% or your annualized savings will increase from $873 to $1,074, or if there is no highway travel, it will decrease accordingly.

- Your motorcycle may have higher or lower average mpg than mine.
- I live in Sacramento CA and average about 20 rain days per year. You may live in a four season area and may only be able to ride your bike 6 months out of the year.
- Your car may have lower average mpg than mine, your motorcycle gas savings would go up.
- Initial cost for both car and motorcycle and the subsequent depreciation must be considered for a true cost comparison.
- Insurance costs for the car do not go away unless the car goes away. My car is idle for 90% of the year but I am still paying insurance and license fees on it all year long. If I lived in a four season area, I could stop insurance on the motorcycle for 6 months per year. What is your particular circumstance?

NOTE: I am only calculating my daily work commute. In the evenings and on the weekends, I use a mix of my motorcycle and my car. Weekly grocery shopping calls for the car to handle all of the grocery bags. Running errands usually means the motorcycle. Unless you are living in a motorcycle only world, you still are going to have a car and the related costs, sitting around the house.

Tips

- Learn your bikes range or how many miles per tank of gas. If you know that you typically have a range of, let's say, 190 miles, you can use this benchmark to validate whatever the gas gauge is saying. For example, your trip meter says you have traveled 175 miles but your gas gauge says you have a half a tank of gas left, you know something doesn't add up. It's time to stop at the next gas station and "fill 'er up".

Bottom Line

You can just skip this math if you like, and simply calculate that a motorcycle has a 50% savings in average mpg. Whatever you are paying for gas in your car today will be reduced by 50% if you were riding a motorcycle instead.

Comfortable or Safe? A Compromise.

About one week after I purchased my brand new Harley Sportster I was out for a Sunday afternoon ride by myself. Except for the 3 day motorcycle course I recently completed, it had been 40 years since I had ridden. I was gun-shy about riding with my wife until I was fairly confident that I would not crash. Apparently, the same standards did not apply to my own safety, go figure.

> Following everything that I had learned about motorcycle safety, I was riding on a hot, 90 degree day. I had my entire Harley recommended gear on. My full face helmet, my full leather jacket (with lining), my lace up hiking boots (I hadn't bought the real "motorcycle" boots yet) and full gloves with cuffs. I was hot. I was really hot. I was dying inside of my self-imposed protective cloak of gear.

> With the sweat rolling down my nose and a little fog on the inside of my face shield, I noticed these other riders in tee-shirts and tennis shoes. They were just having a ball and I just knew they would all crash and burn without all of the proper safety equipment. I may be hot but I was protected, well protected!

I rode like this for the next three months and when I started riding two-up with my wife, I insisted that she do the same. Occasionally, we would stop at the light next to another couple riding in tank tops and skid-lids. We would see them as two people having a great ride and they would see us as newbies, two very well protected newbies.

When we stopped for gas (which was about every 74 miles on the Sportster, by the way), it seemed like we took 10 minutes getting unprotected enough to get out a card to pump gas. Two minutes to top the gas tank off and another 10 minutes to get suited up and continue on to Wal-Mart. And we had not even discovered chaps yet! Thank God!

Six months later, while we never ended up as casual as the tank top and skid lid riders, we had found a happy medium between 100% safe and 0% safe, our own personal "Comfort Zone". We had DOT approved, lightweight NXT half helmets, very comfortable Panoptx glasses, light leather shirts, cool boots and, of course, Levis. I figure we were about 75% as safe as before and about 300% more comfortable. You will find you own "Comfort Zone" somewhere in there also. Life is full of compromise.

Bottom Line

Find the gear that works for you and your riding style. If your gear is just not working for you, do not be afraid to try alternatives. I am not saying to throw safety out the window but I am saying that restrictive and uncomfortable protective gear is a safety hazard in itself. You will discover you're your own riding "comfortable" or riding "safe" compromise.

Resources

DOT	U. S. Department of Transportation	dot.gov
NXT	Out of business taking my $204.95 with them.	nexlsports.com

Safety Statistics

Motorcycle safety is deadly serious. Imagine going outside, putting on your helmet, leather jacket, boots and gloves and then instead of getting on your motorcycle, run across your front yard and when you reach the curb, leap up into the air and land in the street on your chest. (No, don't actually do it, just imagine doing it.) OOF! That's hard. Now imagine the same landing, only at 30 or 40 mph, bouncing again a second and third time. Then imagine landing at 75 mph. Add some altitude and imagine abrasion, broken bones, blood and maybe worst.

Shocked? Do I have you attention yet? Good, because crashing is no fun. Motorcycle safety is deadly serious.

Motorcycles scare the hell out of me!

If reading this stuff puts you off and makes you want to never, ever ride a motorcycle, well that's probably a good thing for you to do. If you are afraid of riding, I believe you will be a high risk rider and you are better off staying in your car.

Personally, I want to know the details. I want to know the odds. I do not want to carry a morbid dread around with me, but I do want to always remember that this ride may be the one that ends up with an unhappy ending. For me, that keeps me focused on what I am doing. And keeping focused is my way of keeping safe. And when I know I am doing everything I can possibly do to ride safely, I enjoy the ride. (Check out my matrix.)

Statistics

I went searching for statistics and I found the National Highway Traffic Safety Administration. After crawling through statistic after statistic, I learned that;

- You are almost twice as likely to be in an accident riding a motorcycle than riding in a passenger car.
- Motorcycle accidents are four times more likely to be deadly than are passenger car accidents.
- There were 69.33 motorcycle fatalities per 100,000 registered motorcycles in 2004. This is a total of 4008 motorcycle fatalities in 2004.

You can check it out for yourself by visiting the NHTSA website.

Additionally:

- More motorcyclist fatalities are occurring on rural roads.
- High (BAC) levels are a major problem among motorcycle operators.
- 1/2 of the fatalities are related to negotiating a curve prior to the crash.
- Over 80 percent of the fatalities occur off roadway.
- Un-divided roadways account for a majority of the fatalities.
- Almost 2/3 of the fatalities were associated with speeding.
- Almost 60 % of motorcyclist fatalities occur at night.
- Collision with a fixed object is a significant factor in over 1/2 of the fatalities.
- Braking and steering maneuvers possibly contribute for almost 25 % of the fatalities.

- Helmet use among fatally injured motorcyclists is below 50 % usage.
- Almost 1/3 of the fatally injured operators did not have a proper license.

So, using these statistics as a guide, if I do not ride my motorcycle on a curved, un-divided, rural road, at night, after drinking, without a helmet, exceeding the speed limit and without a proper motorcycle endorsement on my drivers' license, I will be riding relatively safe.

Seriously though, in the motorcycle rider community, there is a saying, "It's not IF you will go down, it's WHEN you will do down." Everybody eventually goes down and not everybody gets back up again.

Whew, now I'm starting to get depressed. OK, suck it up Frank and get on with it.

Baby boomers have even more at risk. As we get older, bones get more brittle and easier to break. Then they take longer to heal. My sixty year old brain is not as pliable as it was forty years ago and if I get a good hit on my helmet (tree or curb shot), it's going to cause a lot more brain damage to me than to my thirty year old counterparts.

Night vision is an issue but I will assume that if you have a night vision issue, you have already taken steps to correct it.

Dangerous, no question, but look at these statistics;

- In 2005, motorcycle and scooter sales topped the one-million levels for the third straight year. (Motorcycle Industry Council)
- "Back in 1988, the average age for a biker was 32 years old. And in 2005, the average age of a Harley buyer is 48 years old,"

Hmmm, dangerous sport but it seems like more and more folks are riding. What's up with this?

First of all, I like to put it all into my perspective. Don't forget that driving a car comes with its own set of risks. Using a step ladder to change out a light bulb has its risks. Swimming, walking along the side of a road, and in my case, getting the wife mad at me, all can be risky business. There are no guarantees in life and we all choose what level of risk we want to accept by how we live our life.

And secondly, people are riding more every year, in spite of the statistical and real danger involved, because riding a motorcycle is fun. How simple can I be here? Riding a motorcycle is fun.

The ride has an individual allure for each rider. The feeling of freedom, the danger itself, the camaraderie or the almost Zen like tranquility of the ride, (OK, there is the gas mileage and the traffic maneuverability, happy?)

Bottom Line

Some say that motorcycles scare the hell out of them but you know what scares the hell out of me? It's the soccer mom, driving a SUV with a cell phone stuck in her ear. To a motorcycle rider, that is scary!

Resources

National Highway Traffic Safety Administration	Our mission; save lives, prevent injuries, prevent vehicle related accidents.	nrd.nhtsa.dot.gov

Riding Too Conservatively?

We have all been behind the proverbial "little old lady" doing 45 mph in the freeway fast lane. She is like a rock, hanging in there, while the 80 mph stream of cars pass her on the right. Or how about the motor scooter rider who is driving on the shoulder of the road in the bike lane? I cringe whenever I see that and I see more and more of that everyday.

I am a conservative rider but a different kind of conservative rider than these two examples. I absolutely believe in defensive driving (riding), keeping a buffer zone around my motorcycle at all times, using turn signals for every lane change and so on. But I do pay attention to the world around me. Sometimes, you just cannot keep a buffer zone without riding stupid. Trying too hard to stay out of harms way can put you right in the middle of trouble.

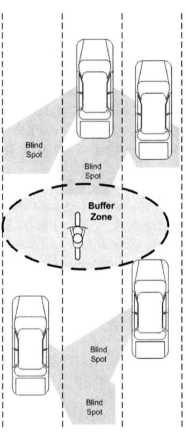

Figure 3 GOOD Buffer Zone

Go With the Flow

If the traffic is running 10 miles per hour over the posted speed limit, then you better speed up and get with it, or get out of it and take another route. When someone is tailgating you hard, move on up and out of the way. Being "in the right" doesn't count when you are laid up in a hospital bed.

When that inevitable 'near death' crisis pops up, the initial reaction is to brake, slow down, avoid whatever it is that is trying to get you. While braking is the initial reaction, don't forget about power and speed as a solution to a close call. Your motorcycle can really go when you want it to so take advantage of it when speed is the appropriate action.

I can't give you a list of specific instances when speed is better than brakes? No can do, just use whatever evasive opportunity that is available, including speed.

Speed vs. Braking

You are in the #3 lane, 60 mph, light traffic, just riding along loving it. In your peripheral vision, you see that SUV in the #1 (or fast) lane, behind you to your left, is suddenly moving across all four lanes in an attempt to make the next exit which is coming up fast. You, of course, are directly in between the SUV and the exit. If you suddenly brake to let the SUV pass in front of you, you may end up on the hood of the car behind you. But if you goose it, and speed up, you can get in front of the SUV's trajectory and let those behind you worry about this jerk. Unexpected lane changes heading your way are good examples of speed getting you out of harms way.

Buffer Zone Speed

Consistently maintaining a buffer zone around you is not easy. Traffic is always changing, tightening up as you approach intersections, getting looser as speed picks up, it's a moving target. You end up next to an erratic driver.

You know it's an erratic driver because you have been paying attention. Your choice is to slow down and still not have a buffer zone or to pick up your speed and get in front, reclaiming your buffer zone.

Outriding Your Skill Level

One last thought is about using speed when you are not skilled enough to do so. I am sure you have heard, "Never outride your skills" and this is a good place to bring that up. When you choose speed, you better be able to handle it. During a crisis is not the time to learn.

I commute to work every day (no rain, thank you) and the last mile or so is through an industrial

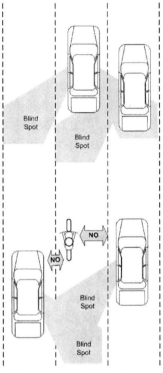

Figure 4 NO Buffer Zone

section with almost no traffic during my 7:00 AM ride. Every day I am testing my skills in this stretch by practicing 45 mpg "push" maneuvers ("push" the right side of the handlebars to go right, "push" the left side to go left) avoiding the imaginary road obstacle such as a 2×4 board, a roofing ladder, a trailer hitch ball, avoiding the imaginary stalled car in the middle of the road and so on.

I have been known to ride through the mall parking lot early Sunday morning when there is not a car in sight and practice figure 8's and tight U-turns. Lock up the brakes at 50 mph and then go back and check out the skid marks.

Imagine what the same maneuvers would be like in the real world.

Bottom Line

I strongly advocate defensive and conservative driving however that does mean you should overlook the speed and power of your bike as an option for taking evasive actions on the road. Never over-ride your skill level and never forget that the inherent nimbleness and speed of your bike is always there available to you.

BASICS

Basic Rider Course

There are a lot of different courses available and they vary from state to state. They may be sponsored by different government agencies. The one you will hear about the most is the MSF course. MSF stands for the Motorcycle Safety Foundation. When someone starts talking about the "Motorcycle Course" this is usually what they are talking about.

Motorcycle Safety Foundation

Here is what they say on their webpage;

> The Motorcycle Safety Foundation® is the internationally recognized developer of the comprehensive, research-based, Rider Education and Training System (MSF RETS). RETS curricula promotes lifelong-learning for motorcyclists and continuous professional development for certified Rider Coaches and other trainers. MSF also actively participates in government relations, safety research, public awareness campaigns and the provision of technical assistance to state training and licensing programs. (Excerpt from the MSF website).

They have a pretty cool webpage by the way that has a ton of information. Also they have a fun "Interactive" motorcycle challenge where you are the driver and you must make some quick decisions on how to handle different traffic problems. Check it out!

There are basic courses, advanced courses and instructor courses available. These courses are most likely offered in your community no matter where you live. Your local motorcycle shop is a good place to get the inside scoop on these classes. Ask them where the courses are offered, where do you sign up? How much do they cost?

Figure 5 MSF Training Class

The Riders Edge® New Rider Course

In addition to the MSF course there's a Harley Davidson version. Also the AMA (American Motorcycle Association) has some good information, check out their website.

MSF Basic Riders Course Review

The MSF Basic course is usually a weekend deal starting with a Friday evening registration class followed by a Saturday and Sunday classroom and hands on riding. There is a test on Sunday at the end of the day. Written test and riding test with no guarantee that you will pass. It's a real test and passing it is a real achievement.

There were about fifteen people in the class that I took, mostly beginners but some very experienced riders in there also. We had two and then three instructors during the course over three days.

MSF provided the motorcycles and helmets. This is a great opportunity to find out what size helmet you head likes. Because these helmets are usually on a donation basis, they had a little bit of everything from just about every manufacturer and size. Spend some time and try a lot of them on. When you find one or two that fit good, write down the details so you have a head start when you are out actually shopping for your own helmet.

Tips

- Oh yeah, make sure to use the helmet liners (a cloth skull cap) to keep all of the cooties off your head from the previous rider students.

You are assigned a small motorcycle, usually a 250 cc street bike. These are not showroom motorcycles but good running even though they have the scars of dozens and dozens of previous student riders on them. It is pretty rare to see any turn signals as they have long ago bitten the dust.

The actual riding activity takes place in a huge parking lot with course outlines made from parking cones. My class was at the local university.

Bottom Line

Why take a safety course? Well, the obvious answer is to learn. Don't be a skeptic; even the seasoned pros learn something in the MSF Basic course. But in addition to the improved skills and knowledge available, graduates of the Basic course may find that there are some licensing test wavers available. I took mine in California and by showing the DMV my MSF certificate, they waved the actual motorcycle driving test. I still had to take the written test but no motorcycle driving test.

Also, most insurance companies offer a monetary discount to graduates of the course, just ask your agent and see what they offer. Hey, it all adds up!

Some dealers and vendors offer discounts to graduates of the course. Look around.

What Does It Cost?

MSF Basic Rider Course	$180 to $300 and sometimes no charge
Riders Edge® New Rider Course	$300 to $350

Resources

Motorcycle Safety Foundation®	Developed the MSF Basic Rider Course along with many more courses.	msf-usa.org
Rider's Edge® New Rider Course	Friendly and approachable, Rider's Edge® program Instructors create a supportive environment that fosters learning and interaction. ...	ridersedge.com

Starter Bikes

I am going to go with the assumption that you are interested in riding a cruiser. Not a BMW, Goldwing, Sports Bike or dirt bike but a cruiser. I don't have anything against all of the other styles of motorcycles, it's just that I ride a cruiser and my experience, and this book is focused on a cruiser.

I need to warn all of you dyed in the wool, Harley, buy American, never ride a rice-burner folks to get ready as I am about to offend your sensitive side. I am going to recommend that the beginning or re-entry, riders, go out and buy a Japanese cruiser for a started bike.

Japanese Cruiser

Yes folks, a Japanese cruiser, 250cc to 450cc, relatively light and easy to handle, a starter bike. I say starter bike because, if you start riding and come to a profound decision that this motorcycle riding business sucks, you do not have $10 to $20 thousand hanging out there on a Harley purchase. Plus that, once you figure in the Harley Tax (Oh, you haven't heard about that yet?) Dealer prep charges, sales tax, drive-it-off-the-lot depreciation, and you can add another $4 or $5 thousand to that total.

Here are three examples I pulled from eBay in a no-brainer five minute search. All three of these will probably sell between $1500 and $2500. Not that cheap but remember, even an entry level Sportster will cost over three times that amount.

- 1999 Suzuki, GS GZ-250, 11000 mi., 250 cc
- 2003 Honda, Rebel, 3348 mi., 250 cc
- 1995 Yamaha, Virago 250, 6010 mi., 250 cc

- 1984 Honda, Magna, 5830 mi., 500 cc

Don't be hesitant because of the smaller engine size (250 cc − 500 cc), these bikes are a lot lighter than their big brothers and lot easier to handle.

Try It and See If You Like It

The idea is to find out if you are really that excited about riding. These bikes will get you into traffic, offer an easier learning curve and let you find out if you like all of this without getting too committed.

If you plan on riding with your significant other, best friend or just hoping to get lucky, make sure you buy a bike that already has seating for two. You don't want to start investing money into this motorcycle because you will have a difficult time getting it back when you sell it. Buying a new seat or exhaust is not cheap and when you are looking at a 90 day assessment period, just leave everything stock and ride it.

Private party is usually the way to go. Do not be surprised if the seller will not let you take it for a test ride. Put yourself in their place, you will be letting somebody you don't know, hop on your motorcycle for an around the block ride and you may never see them again. Be patient and if they will not let you ride it, ask them to ride it while you follow them in the car looking to see if the bike tracks straight, accelerates without a lot of smoke and just general performance.

If it is possible, have a motorcycle mechanic check it out. Let the seller ride it to the neighborhood cycle shop and pay the mechanic $50 to make sure you are not buying someone's nightmare. If no mechanic is available, spend some time taking a good look at the machine. Here is a simple checklist that will help you to make sure you do not overlook anything.

Table 1. Used Bike Condition Checklist

Brakes, disc/ pads	Worn, scarred, metal to metal? Last changed?
Controls	All working? Non-stock, crashed?
Engine Sound	Smooth rev, no valve noise, odd noises,
Exhaust	Discolored chrome (carburetor problems), smoking (valves), exhaust pressure same on both pipes?
Fluids	Oil is clean, no metal? Synthetic?
Frame	Cracks, modifications, bent, straight?
Gas Tank	Rust? Milky colored gas?
Hoses	Leaks, cracks, connectors look good?
Lights	Working, bright, steady? (fluctuate with engine revs may be charger problems)
Paperwork	Maintenance records/receipts, VIN matches registration, mileage correct
Starter	Strong start?
Tires	Cracked sidewalls (old), pressure OK?, valve stem in straight (tube shifting)
Wiring	Cracked, unusual colored wire (what happened to the original wire)

My advice, buy a cheap starter bike to find out if riding a motorcycle is what you really want to do.

Scooters

Scooters, hey, I thought this book was about motorcycles, not scooters. Scooters have come a long way, baby. My 1960's "Nifty, Thrifty, Honda 50" has migrated into today's super class of scooters like the Suzuki Burgman. This Suzuki Burgman has a 650cc, fuel-injected motor and electronically controlled, continuously variable transmission, scooter. It weighs 518 pounds and is a freeway machine with a top speed of 115 mph. It will set you back over $10,000 brand new.

- Classic Motorscooter (50cc – 60cc) is the style most people think about when they envision a motorscooter.
- Basic Motorscooter (50cc to 150cc) includes the Classic and may be highway compatible.
- Performance Motorscooter (150cc to 250cc) refers to the increased engine performance and may be called a racing motorscooter.
- Touring Motorscooters (150cc to 250 cc or higher) are built with passengers in mind, have sound systems and range up to the high end Suzuki Burgman in highway compatibility.

Figure 6 Suzuki Burgman

I have put in a lot of miles on scooters as a young man and there are some scooter pluses and minuses. On the plus side, they are inexpensive and very easy to handle. Parking and moving around in city traffic is a breeze. For some folks, not needing to swing your leg up and over to get on is a real benefit. On the negative side, too many people treat riding a scooter like riding a bicycle. They do not use protective gear, they ride on the shoulder of the road and in general, they are just too casual about riding the scooter. That asphalt is just as hard and unforgiving to a scooter rider as it is to a motorcycle rider and if you are not safety conscious, the results can be disastrous.

Scooters may be just what you are looking for depending on your particular riding needs. Personally, I am not a big fan of scooters just like I am not a big fan of sport-bikes and touring bikes. It is just my personal preference.

Always Buy Quality Personal Protective Gear

Keep in mind that if it's a cheap Japanese cruiser or if it's the real-deal Harley, buying your personal riding gear is an independent thing. Your personal riding gear, (helmet, leather, boots, etc.) doesn't care how much the motorcycle cost when you hit the pavement and are sliding along at 40 mph, so buy quality stuff, that fits, and will be there for you when you need it. Don't be surprised if you spend $1500 on a motorcycle and then spend even MORE on your personal rider gear.

Bottom Line

Until you are 100% certain that riding a motorcycle is what you enjoy, buy an inexpensive bike, a Japanese cruiser to start. Buy it used from a private party and spend the money to have it checked out by an experienced motorcycle mechanic. And finally, when you buy your personal protective gear, buy quality. Shop around for the best price but do not compromise on the quality.

What Does It Cost?

Harley Davidson Sportster	$12,000 new
Harley Davidson Softtail	$18,000 new
Japanese cruiser, 250cc to 450cc	$1,000 to $3,000 used
Basic Motorscooter (50cc to 150cc)	$2,500 to $4,500 new

Resources

eBay	On-Line Auction	motors.ebay.com
Harley Davidson	American motorcycle manufacturer	harley-davidson.com
Honda	Japanese motorcycle manufacturer	powersports.honda.com
Suzuki	Japanese motorcycle manufacturer	suzukicycles.com
Yamaha	Japanese motorcycle manufacturer	yamaha-motor.com

Insurance

No, don't skip this chapter. It is a short chapter but an important one. I will not bore you to tears with actuary stuff like it depends upon your driving record, your age, where you live and blah, blah, blah. I will tell you some interesting motorcycle insurance stuff. Keep in mind that I am not an insurance agent. I don't own any interests in any insurance business. I am just a consumer just like you. And I don't know about you but I personally hate everything about insurance. Here is the interesting stuff.

Shop Around

I know, you have heard it over and over again but it's really true with insurance companies. Not all insurance companies "get it" when it comes to motorcycles. I will wager if you call five different insurance companies, you will get 5 quotes that have over a $1,000 spread in the price. Same coverage, just some insurance companies think motorcycles are cars.

Go ahead and Google "motorcycle insurance" and choose the companies that say they deal specifically with motorcycles. OK, that move alone just saved about $500 per year. That was easy, eh?

Coverage

Now, it's up to you and the state you live in on what amounts of coverage you want to get. I personally want to get coverage that does all of the normal personal liability and so on but I want motorcycle specific coverage.

- I want the motorcycle to be replaced if it is totaled or stolen. I want a 100% no-hassle replacement.

- I want the replacement settlement to include the $2,000 (or $20,000) worth of aftermarket gear and equipment I have on the motorcycle. Yes, they will cover this. They will want to see receipts and proof that all of this stuff was actually on the motorcycle.
- I don't care about rental cars, hotel reimbursements or towing. I have the HD HOG member roadside package for $50 per year that covers all of that stuff. I am especially concerned about the towing. You don't tow a motorcycle like you tow a car, you lift it on a hoist and swing it over onto the rear of the tow truck so it does not become damaged (or more damaged) in transit. I don't want my bike lying on its side in the back of a tow truck for a 50 mile freeway ride.
- I want a 10% discount for the MSF training I received.

Where do I keep my proof of insurance papers?

Good question. Some states require you to keep your registration and proof of insurance on the bike itself. The others just want you to have it with you and available upon demand. I live in California and here you just need to have it available. I like this as I do not really want my papers on the bike in case someone steals the bike. Maybe I'm just paranoid but if they steal the bike, I don't want to help them out with any additional information.

If you do keep the papers with the bike, there are some options on how to do this.

Tips
- Make sure to keep your papers in a waterproof (sandwich bag) enclosure so the rain does not find them.
- Make a Xerox copy and keep it at home.

My Suzuki Intruder 1400 had a sissy bar with a built in tool compartment which made a great place for these papers. Many bikes have the same. Be creative.

Most saddlebags have a pocket inside of them just for these papers. If you have detachable bags, you will always need to remember to take the papers out of the bag when you leave the bags at home.

You can purchase an add-on metal tube that has a screw on cap and is waterproof. You roll up your papers and slide them into this tube. This tube can be attached anywhere you like on your bike. Most folks attaché it to the top 2 bolts that hold on your license plate. The

Figure 7 Registration Tube

downside is that anyone else can unscrew the tube cap and grab your papers.

Another clever option is an add-on waterproof storage box that is the same size as your license plate, ½"to 1" thick and is placed behind your license plate. It is difficult to see and different models have different screw techniques to secure the box.

Bottom Line

I sincerely hope that my insurance policy will never need to be actually used, but if I do need it, I want to walk away from it all with the same ride and all of the stuff I started out with.

OK, that's it, lets go have fun.

What Does It Cost?

Motorcycle Insurance	Varies but usually less than car insurance
HD HOG member roadside package	$50 annually

Resources

Harley Davidson Roadside Assistance	Various towing, rental cars, hotel reimbursements packages	harley-davidson.com

Counter-Steering: Push the Handlebars

Push right, go right and push left, go left is the technique you use on a motorcycle that is moving faster than 5 mph. Under 5 mph, the motorcycle steers just like a bicycle.

On a bicycle when you want to go to the right, you turn the front wheel to the right. Usually you do this by pulling on the right hand side of the handlebars. The bicycle goes right and you are in business. On a motorcycle, this is the same when you are traveling at very low speeds, under 5 mph.

Once your motorcycle speed up past 5 mph, the laws of physics come into play. Your wheels become gyroscopes and create their own gyroscopic motion or force. The faster you go, the more powerful this gyroscopic force becomes.

Now when you want to go to the right, you push on the right side of the handlebars. Yes, it's all backwards from a bicycle. Conversely, when you want to go to the left, you push on the left side of the handlebars. You push on the left handgrip. This will make your motorcycle go to the left.

In the MSF Basic Rider course, you will be taught:

Push Right, Go Right and Push Left, Go Left

This is all backwards from your natural urge to pull right to go right. This is why this technique is called counter-steering. You are steering counter to your natural instincts.

This sounds goofy but is really is not very hard to get the hang of it. After your 8 hours of riding during the MSF Basic Rider course, you are dialed in to this and it probably has already become a habit, a learned skill.

In practical application you will use the low speed (under 5 mph) bicycle style of just turning the handlebars to go where you want to go. Once you are at speed, the push technique comes into play. I mention that I often practice this when I find myself on an empty road. I practice avoiding an imaginary road hazard.

Practice Makes Perfect

I imagine that the upcoming sewer cover in the middle of my lane is a road obstacle like a dead skunk, a metal trailer ball or a 2X4 piece of wood. As I approach this sewer cover, I will swerve around it to the left and immediately swerve back into my original line or track. I push the left handgrip to swerve to the left and then immediately push the right handgrip to swerve to the right and get back on my original line.

The skill part that I am practicing is to do this maneuver very quickly at the last second prior to riding over the sewer cover.

The practical application part of this is simulating what really happens on the highway. On no traffic roads, you can see any upcoming obstacle well in advance and can gradually ride around it. In traffic, road obstacles do not become apparent until the car directly in front of you passed over them and you are next in line to do the same. If you are following good practice and riding in the left car tire tract, you will see the obstacle and already be on a lie to avoid it. If you are riding between the cart tracks, or if the car in front of you clips the object and moves it into your line, you must take some pretty quick evasive action.

Push left (or right) to avoid the obstacle and then immediately push in the opposite direction to get back on your line. That is what I am practicing. Although this has become second nature to me, I believe I keep it second nature by practicing when ever I have an opportunity. In the real world, you may not need to avoid some obstacle in the road for several weeks or even months but when the need arises, it is usually right now.

Bottom Line

Push Right, Go Right and Push Left, Go Left works when your motorcycle is traveling over 5 mph. This skill is one that you must keep ready at all times.

Go Where You Look

Understanding this concept is another critical piece of the riding puzzle. Go where you look means that, when riding, you (and your motorcycle) will go to wherever you are looking. The formal term for this is "Target Fixation". Here are three examples;

- When you see a pothole coming up and you stare at it while you are approaching it, odds are that you will hit it.
- Making a tight U-turn on a residential street and halfway through the turn you look at the opposing curb, odds are that you will hit the curb.
- During a gradual turn on a two lane road, you look at the oncoming traffic; odds are that you will ride right into oncoming traffic.

Sounds crazy, it did to me at first, but I am here to tell you that it is the truth. In each of these three examples, as soon as you realize you are heading into a problem, immediately look away from the pothole, curb and the oncoming traffic and look at where you really want to go. (If you are not too far into the pending collision, changing your look will change your direction in time to avoid the imminent crash.)

Looking at the spot that you are trying to avoid will suck you into that spot every time. Looking at the spot where you do want to go, will move your motorcycle towards that spot.

You have experienced this in a car before when you are looking at the passing scenery and your car starts drifting over the road in the direction you are looking.

This was hard for me to overcome as I am always trying to look at that pothole (for example). I must force myself to look away from the pothole and look where I do want to go, typically, around the pothole. They say that once you see the pothole, keep it in your peripheral vision but focus your main vision on the desired direction or spot of your intended travel. That goes for any upcoming road hazard, keep it in your peripheral vision and look at the path or spot where you want to go.

Look where you go in a sloping gradual turn, look at the vanishing point of the turn, the end of the turn. If you want to take the turn closer to the side of the road, look even further past the end of the turn and you will travel closer to the edge of the road.

Now, none of this look where you go stuff is completely automatic, you still are in charge of driving the motorcycle. You still must use all of your riding skills to make the motorcycle go where you want it to go and looking where you go will ensure that you get to where you want to go.

Conversely, some riders can get fixed on looking at a certain spot and no matter how hard they try, they just can't seem to snap their look away or move the motorcycle in a different direction. If this is you, please pay attention to this phenomenon. Practice make perfect and some folks (like me) must practice all of the time.

Then there are other folks who have a natural knack for this and just jump on their bike and ride with everything falling into place just like a natural skill.

Get out in that empty parking lot and practice avoiding some potholes (or just different colored asphalt patches in the lot. If you can, place some orange traffic cones and weave thru them using your peripheral vision on the cones and your main vision on the path you want to take.

Bottom Line

Looking where you want to go is a reality of motorcycle riding. You must master this before you get out into the traffic. Does that mean putting in 10,000 miles in a parking lot first? No, but it does mean that you absolutely must understand this and do it enough so you get the feel for it. Do not wait until you are in a critical traffic maneuver to learn how to go where you are looking.

Friction Zone

Understanding the correct use of the "Friction Zone" is one of the most powerful riding techniques that you will have in your riding skill set. I thought I knew what the friction zone was but I really did not understand it at first and more importantly, I did not know how to use it when riding.

Friction Zone

So what the heck is all the fuss about? What is the friction zone? The friction zone is a part of the clutch engagement and disengagement process. I am assuming as you read this that you know how to shift gears on a motorcycle (or a car with a manual transmission). You pull in the clutch (disengage), shift gears and then release (disengage) the clutch. You repeat this process as you shift you way up and down through the gears on your motorcycle. That is how a clutch works in the simplest terms.

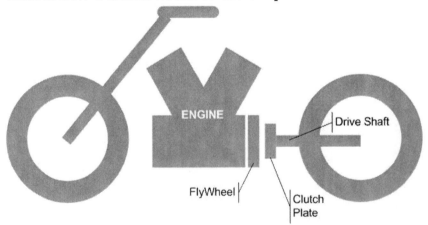

Figure 8 Where is the clutch plate and flywheel?

But what is actually happening inside your motorcycle when you engage and disengage your clutch. There are two rotating shafts in your bike, one is rotated by the engine and is called the flywheel. The other rotating shaft is what transfers power to the rear wheel of your bike and is called the drive shaft.

If you are always in gear, never shifting or stopping, both shafts could be hooked together and would not even need a clutch. However, you do need to stop now and then and when your machine is stopped; the rear wheel must be disconnected from the engine. This allows the engine to keep running while the rear wheel is not moving. The clutch is between the flywheel and the driveshaft and it is the clutch engaging and disengaging which connects these two shafts together or disconnects and takes them apart. When the clutch is engaged, the engine power is transferred to the rear wheel. When the clutch is disengaged, the power stays with the engine and the rear wheel has no power. The engine and rear wheel become independent from each other.

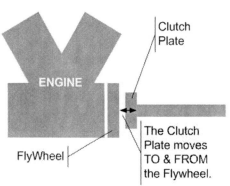

Figure 9 Clutch plate and flywheel

OK, so what is the friction zone? Hold on, I am getting there. The important thing or concept to understand is that the clutch is what applies power to the rear wheel. And you need to visualize how the clutch is performing this magic.

The engine flywheel is a heavy circular metal plate that revolves faster and slower as the engine speed is increased and decreased. Next to the flywheel is the clutch plate which is also a circular metal disc attached to the driveshaft. They are next to each other just like two pieces of bread in a sandwich but they are not touching each other. The sandwich is keeping the two pieces of bread apart with peanut butter and jelly while the clutch plate is kept apart from the flywheel with a controlled air gap. Your hand clutch level is what controls this air gap.

When your hand clutch lever is fully released, there is no air gap and the clutch plate is fully engaged or firmly pressed against the flywheel. This union, this pressure union, is how the engine power gets transferred from the engine to the driveshaft and the driveshaft turns the rear wheel.

When you hand clutch level is pulled up tight against the handlebar handgrip, the clutch is fully released or disengaged. This means that the engine is unconnected from the driveshaft and can rev up and down independent of the rear wheel.

Are you with me here? If not, read it again.

LEVER OUT

CLUTCH ENGAGED

LEVER IN

CLUTCH DIS-ENGAGED

OK, now we can talk about the friction zone. Your bikes clutch lever and control is designed with a lot of extra play in it. It needs to compensate for things getting worn out over time, temperature swings and a bunch of stuff. By the time your clutch lever has reached it outermost position, the

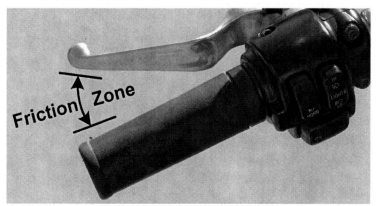

Figure 10 Clutch Lever Friction Zone

clutch has already been engaged. By the time your clutch level reaches its innermost position against the handlebar grip, your clutch has already been disengaged. So, lets say that your clutch level has a 3" travel distance from all the way out to all the way in, probably all of the clutch engagement and disengagement action is taking place in 1 ½ inches of that 3 inch travel distance.

This 1 ½ inches is where the clutch plate starts to touch the flywheel and continues touching it until it is firmly rotating at the same speed as the flywheel. To you the rider, without seeing all of this clutch action going on, you must depend upon your sense of feel to know the clutch is engaging and disengaging.

As you pull the clutch in, you will feel the power start to disappear from the rear wheel. As you let it out, the power starts returning to the back wheel. And this, my friend, is the friction zone.

I hope you got it because it isn't over yet. Now you know what the friction zone is. Let me restate it one more time.

The friction zone is the clutch process from when the clutch plate first touches the flywheel, onward until it is fully engaged and the backward until it is fully released and is no longer touching the flywheel. They call it the friction zone because friction is how the faster flywheel couples with the slower clutch plate and starts transferring power.

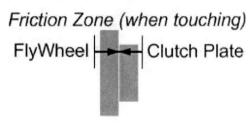

Figure 11 Friction Zone

Congratulations, you made it. You now know what the friction zone is and I have not yet told you a thing about how you can use it to your advantage.

Slow Speeds Are Where the Friction Zone Works Best

Low speeds, less than 5 mph, are the most difficult speeds for maneuvering your motorcycle. Higher speeds have those wonderful forces of nature, centrifugal force and momentum to help keep you upright and in control. But at the lower speeds it's all about pure balance. The lower the speed, the more challenging it becomes to keep the motorcycle vertical. Low enough speed and you are simply walking your motorcycle around the place.

As you decrease your speed, 15 mph, 10 mph, 5 mph, you hit a point where the engine is at its lowest RPM, but it is too much power for the rear wheel and you start pulling the clutch to allow the rear wheel to revolve slower than the engine.

You simply must pull in the clutch or your engine will die. With the clutch engaged at these low speeds your engine simply cannot slow down enough to match the low revolutions of your rear wheel. Now, using the friction zone to your advantage, you can fine tune how much clutch is actually engaging the flywheel. Now you can really control how much power is applied to the rear wheel, keeping the rear wheel under power without killing the engine.

Stop and Go Traffic

The simplest application is when you are stuck in stop and go traffic. Every time you move forward ten feet and get your feet re-planted on the ground, the car in front of you move up another ten feet. This goes on, over and over again. Using the friction zone, you can ride forward, letting the clutch slip off the higher engine revolutions and stay under power. When you are still under power, even if it's only a part of the power, you have much more control over your bike.

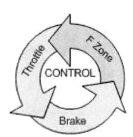

Figure 12 Secret of Low Speed Control

Now let's take it one step further. You are using the friction zone to keep the rear wheel under power and now you <u>additionally</u> start riding (applying) the rear brake. Yes, that's it, the clutch is playing the friction zone, the throttle is controlling the rear wheel power and the rear brake is controlling your forward stop and go progress. This sounds way more complicated that it really is. Clutch, throttle and brake are all working in concert to keep you in control of your bike.

Depending upon the time duration between each stop and go, you may even be able to just keep riding without stopping.

Caution: Practice this technique in an empty parking lot, away from traffic. You will be surprised how quickly you catch on and how much more control you will have over you bike when you are under 5 mph. Practice make perfect so keep at it until you are comfortable before you try this out in the traffic.

U-Turns on a Narrow Residential Street

This is another low speed maneuver where using the friction zone will really make a difference. Without using the friction zone, you are a circus balancing act with the U-turn radius so small, your speed is so low, and you find yourself placing all of your focus on just keeping the bike from tipping over and no focus on what you are doing. This difficult low speed maneuver really becomes quite manageable with the rear wheel under power. You are using all three tools, friction zone, throttle and rear brake. Try it out. You will be absolutely amazed at the additional control all of this will give you in these difficult low speed maneuvers.

Parking Lot Maneuvers

Same deal, in and out of one tight squeeze after another. Next time when you are sitting in traffic in your car and you see some motorcycle carefully and slowly coming up from behind, splitting lanes, take a look at the riders clutch hand and brake foot. You will see the experienced riders doing exactly what I am telling you. Friction zone, throttle and rear brake will open a new riding skill level to you and really improve your motorcycle riding enjoyment.

CAUTION: Using your front brake at speeds under 5 miles per hour will suck your motorcycle to the ground like a magnet. Personally, I rely solely on the rear brake at these low speeds.

Bottom Line

Understand the friction zone, understand how the machine works and then apply this knowledge to your ride. Clutch, throttle and brake is a powerful combination that gives you total control over your motorcycle. Learn it, use it and enjoy it.

Improving the Odds

When I re-entered the world of motorcycles, I was driven by a desire to enjoy my life and have fun. Knowing the danger inherent in motorcycle riding, I did my homework on safety. I took the MSF course, I read everything I could find, I talked to experienced riders, and I really did my homework. And after all of this it was only after about 10,000 miles that I had refined my initial view of safety down to the following three things which (in my humble opinion) make or break the safety element;

1. Mechanical condition of your bike
2. Ride within your ability
3. Focus on the ride

If you pay attention to these three things, you will have significantly improved the odds. You will have eliminated three areas of potential risk. You can only get better by constantly learning, practicing and keeping these three elements up to speed. All three of these will become habit after a short period of really doing them correctly. Once you are there however, you cannot let go and drift into carelessness.

Bottom Line

Riding a motorcycle is fun. Go have some fun.

Mechanical condition of the motorcycle

A flat tire on a car can be dangerous but a flat tire on a motorcycle can be flat out life threatening. My point is that mechanical problems on a motorcycle can be magnitudes greater than mechanical problems on a car. You really need to keep your machine in top operating condition. That does not mean it must be ready for a motorcycle show, gleaming, spotless and looking like it just rolled off the showroom floor. It can need a bath, have 800 miles of bugs plastered on it, and the only shinny place is where you place your backside on the seat.

It just needs to be in good operating condition.

TCLOCK

"TCLOCK" is the Motorcycle Safety Foundation's pre-ride inspection. If you spend some time and learn this, whenever you get ready to ride, just remember "TCLOCK" and do your check.

T	Tires
C	Controls
L	Lights & Accessories
O	Oils & Fluids
C	Chassis & Chain
K	Kickstand

Figure 13 TCLOCK

Tires: Tire pressure is critical. Overinflating or under inflating the tires can make your ride uncomfortable and the handling poor. I carry a tire pressure gauge in my "Sausage Bag" which is almost always strapped onto my rear fender rack. I have a second one in my tool bag on the front forks but because my tool bag is time consuming to open (what, 30 seconds?), I almost never use it. I don't trust the gauge built into the air machine at the corner gas station. It is rarely accurate. How critical is this? On my HD Wide Glide, I can feel 2 or 3 pounds of air pressure difference on the front tire as I ride.

Additionally, regular air pressure checking will alert you to a slow leak and let you fix it on your terms, not on a long ride in a strange town with the weather starting to turn nasty as the sun goes down and the night creatures start roaming the highways (I'm starting to freak myself out here.).

Controls: Check the throttle, clutch and both brakes. Do this with the engine off so you can hear any alien noises which may be a tip off to trouble. Roll the bike forward and backward to actually make the brakes work. If you hear any snap-crackle-pop or grinding, check it out real close.

Lights and accessories: Yes, you need to test them all. Check your right and left turn signals, front and rear, your headlight, high and low beam. When I am alone, I will back my bike up to a car or wall so I can see the rear brake light flash on and off using the reflection of the car or wall. Just because it was working the last time you checked doesn't mean it's working today. Don't forget your horn.

Oils and fluids: When you check your oil, remember that until the engine has been running, all of the oil has settled to the bottom of the crankcase overnight and your oil dipstick will have a higher reading. At lease start the engine and let the oil pump circulate the oil before you check the level.

Check your brake fluid through the window on the handlebar reserve. And do not forget to check the gas. Running out of gas is really a hassle and it gets worst if you are pushing your 650 pound bike while mentally kicking yourself for not checking before you ran out of gas. Ouch!

Chassis and chain: What chain? Hey, it makes the acronym work (TCLOCK) so check it. Take a look at the chassis, really take a look. No you do not need to put the motorcycle on a lift or lie on the ground, just focus on what you are looking at when you look. Stop daydreaming and check for broken welds, new damage, tight bolts and so on. You should be able to give it the once-over in 30 seconds or less.

Kickstand: Just check and make sure that when you stand the bike up straight and kick up the kick stand, the kickstand retracts tightly to the bottom of the frame. You do not want any low hanging kickstands. A lot of bikes have a contact kill switch in place that will kill the engine when the kickstand is lowered.

Trust Your Mechanic

Trust your mechanic (even if it is yourself).

I took my Suzuki Intruder 1400 into the Suzuki shop in Reno complaining that the rear brake was spongy and slow to respond. Their "Ace" mechanic rode it around the parking lot, took a close look at the rear brake disc and announced that everything was normal for a "cruiser". They all are spongy and slow due to the weight.

I rode off going to Carson City, 30 miles down the road. Just outside of Carson City, the 70 mph highway turned into a 35 mph city street and when I tried to slow down, I had no rear brakes. I stopped (front brake was good, thank you) and checked out the rear brake. The disc was faintly red from friction and so hot I actually was worried that the brake would burst into flames.

The mechanic in the Carson City Suzuki dealership took a look and told me that the disc was warped like a hubcap, not flat, so the brake pads have bee rubbing and that's where the heat buildup happened. He asked me if I had not noticed the rear brakes becoming sluggish and unresponsive. My point is you must find a good mechanic who you trust.

Use the TCLOCK before you go for a ride. In the bigger picture, proper maintenance will end up being less expensive than on-demand maintenance. Don't let your bike slide into poor condition. Keep it up just like your life depends on it, because, it does.

Ride within your ability

Statistically, a lot of motorcycle accidents are lone rider accidents. No car involved, just a lone rider crashing. Riding beyond your ability results in things like;

- Overshooting the curve because you came in too fast and are unable to correct without going down. You end up on the wrong side of the road riding right into the traffic of the edge of the road.
- Inexperienced splitting lanes and just generally riding too aggressive for your skill level can bring you down in traffic with disastrous results.
- Wet roads, loose gravel and just plain leaves on the road require experienced riding. Some of this experience can only be obtained by making mistakes. Practice in an empty parking lot, not on the road.

So how do I know if I am riding within my ability? That's a tough question. I mean it's easy to know when you have exceeded your ability by the immediate results (crash bang boom) but staying within your ability is a lot different.

No Riding Loss of Ability

For example, I commute to work 40 miles each day in city traffic. I practice all of my own safety rules, I ride conservatively but I do ride like I am on a motorcycle. That means I take advantage of my smaller vehicle profile to go where I could not go in a car. I am comfortable, I feel safe and I am confident that I am within my ability. However after a six week layoff during the winter (California style winter, rain) when I start riding again, I can really feel that my ability has gone soft during the six week lay off. I am not as quick; I spend a lot more time thinking about the motorcycle which means less time thinking about the traffic. It takes me several weeks until I feel like I am back in charge.

When I feel like I am back in charge, I am not thinking about "looking where I want to go", I am just doing it. I am going into the turn at just the right speed that allows me to slightly accelerate (roll on the throttle) during the curve and come out the other end of the curve solid and ready for the next road change.

At a traffic light, I am watching the cross traffic, the pedestrians, the cars next to me and when the light turns green, I am moving with the flow. Not any jack rabbit starts, no surprises. I am riding within my ability.

Bottom Line

I think you will know the second you exceed your ability. You suddenly feel some loss of control. I don't mean you can not control the bike but you lose your power over the bike. You find yourself making immediate adjustments to regain your control (power) over the bike. You slow down; move over into a slower lane, you do something. When you experience this, you are learning you limits of riding ability.

Focus

Focus on what you are doing which is riding.

One of the focus theories which I have read is about starting out your ride with $10 worth of focus. Each distraction, takes away from this focus. Low on gas subtracts $1 leaving you $9 worth of focus. Boots are too tight and hurting your feet, subtract another $2; engine is running rough, running rough, another $2 so now you are down to $5 worth of focus.

I like this analogy, you always want to have $10 worth of focus and you need to eliminate the distractions which are taking away from the $10 goal.

Sometimes in a car, every driver out there experiences a loss of focus. They may drive 20 miles on the turnpike thinking about their job or marriage and not even remember traveling those 20 miles. This is a luxury you just can not afford when riding a motorcycle. You must remain focused on what you are doing.

Statistically, most accidents happen within 5 miles of your home. Well that makes sense; after all you are always departing and arriving from the same location. All of your short rides fall within this tight perimeter. One trick that will help you keep your focus is to always think like you are going 50 miles no matter how short the ride. When you are thinking 50 miles, you seem to make a little more effort to make sure you have all of the proper riding gear on. You ride like you are in it for a longer time, not so much just hot-rodding around. You will have a more stable attitude about the ride.

In the movies, I see the motorcycle rider cruising down the main drag, head weaving back and forth checking out everyone who is walking down the street. Waving and shouting hellos over the shoulder to people they know. It's a beautiful world, just out enjoying the ride.

In the real non-movie world which we mortals must live in, that over the shoulder hello to a pedestrian, results in looking forward and seeing the back of a truck stopped ten feet in front of you and you are still going 30 mph. Ouch! Loss of focus is a hard lesson.

Here's some more statistics. Most riders go down during their first six months of riding when they are still learning. But, in years two and three, there are even more riders going down because they think they know everything and lose focus. Now that's something to think about.

Bottom Line

Make sure your motorcycle is mechanically sound, ready for duty, stay within your riding ability limits and always keep your focus on what you are doing, on the ride.

Resources

"$10 worth of focus"	Twist of the Wrist: The Motorcycle Road Racers Handbook by Keith Code	ISBN-13: 978-0965045018
Motorcycle Safety Foundations	Developed the MSF Basic Rider Course along with many more courses.	msf-usa.org

They Can't Hit You if You're Not There

Well, duh Frank, of course they can't hit you if you're not there but I have to ride in the real world and they are there, all of the time. I have to share the road with cars, trucks, buses, bicycles and anything else that happens along.

I understand, what I mean is to keep yourself (and your bike) positioned out of the danger zone. Don't ride in some cars blind spot. Don't ride next to any vehicle. Don't ride behind a big truck. I realized that this is only possible in a perfect world, but you can make every effort to stay out of danger's path even in the real world.

Cars hit motorcycles because the car's driver can't see the motorcycle. Either the motorcycle is in the cars blind spot or the car's driver is just not paying attention. Adjust your speed to stay out of the blind spot and flash you headlights when you need to get their attention.

Car Blind Spot

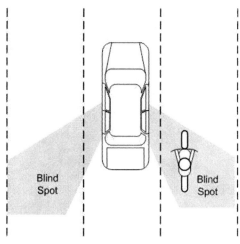

Figure 14 Car Blind Spot

Let's take a look at the blind spot first. Every car has blind spots, some more, some less. When you are in a car blind spot, you are at even more risk that just the average driver's lack of "looking" whenever they change lanes. At speed (freeway) this can result in a very quick evasive maneuver for you, the motor cycle rider.

But at even street speeds, cars changing lanes into you are a critical risk. Stay out of these blind spots whenever possible. Speed up, slow down, change lanes, do whatever is reasonable to stay out of the blind spots. Like I said, if you aren't there, they can't hit you.

Truck Blind Spot

The risk is multiplied as more and more cars join you on the road. More cars, more blind spots and fewer alternative places to be and stay safely out of the blind spots.

Stay away from trucks. That's it, simple, stay away from trucks. When circumstances force you to ride near a truck, I suggest you treat the entire truck as a blind spot.

It gets back to the focus thing. Stay focused; actively ride into the safe zones. When you have no choice but to be in a

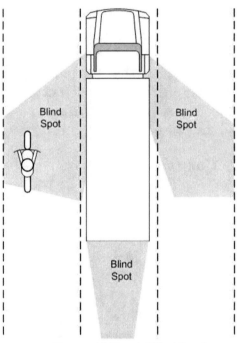

Figure 15 Truck Blind Spot

blind spot, get through it quickly, don't just ride along with the flow of traffic placing your safety on the hands of some driver thinking about the rising price of gas.

Coupled with the blind spot awareness is the constant effort to be aware of erratic drivers. You know who I mean. You see them at the stop light shuffling through their briefcase and papers, slow to go when the light turns green. The soccer mom with a cell phone to her ear and a SUV full of noisy kids is another alarm going off in your head. The cool guy in the fast and furious, ground effects Honda with the popcorn exhaust driving everyone crazy is going to move into your lane when you least expect it. You just know these drivers are dangerous and they will change lanes like it's a video game in their living room. Once you have spotted these drivers, stay clear. Don't just avoid their blind spot, get out in front of them or pull back and get three or four cars behind them. There is a traffic accident waiting to happen and you do not want to participate.

Have you ever been creeping along in traffic and had a motorcycle come blasting past you, splitting lanes between you and the next car? Their arrival and departure is so fast, and the shock of hearing the exhaust sounds just make you want to jump right out of your seat. How did you not see them coming? How could they get so close, so fast, and simply surprise you? Well, they probably are going too fast and all of that but I will guarantee you that your blind spot helped camouflage their arrival.

Now put yourself on that offending motorcycle and think about it. What will happen when you scare some car driver and they instinctively crank the wheel right into you? I do not have anything against splitting lanes but just because it's legal (in some states anyway), you still need to use your common sense when you are doing it.

Same scenario only now you are on a motorcycle when a second motorcycle passes you, in your lane, right next to you, and scares the dickens out of you. You never saw them coming and your initial, automatic reaction is to change lanes and get away from this rocket as fast as possible. Fortunately for you, by the time you can actually react, the second motorcycle is gone and the only thing hurt is your pride. Keep one eye on your rear view mirror and don't let anything coming up from behind surprise you. If you are riding a Sportster of some other mirror vibrating, "can't see anything" motorcycle. Get the mirrors fixed so you can see behind you or get another motorcycle. You must always be aware of your immediate surroundings so you can take evasive actions on a reflex basis.

They can't hit you if your not there applies to rear-end accidents. This is just plain old defensive driving. Sitting at the light, always keep an eye on your rearview mirror. Are they going to stop? Are they just going to slam into you? Pump your brake lights, keep it in gear and always leave enough room between you and the car in front of you for some quick evasive action. When in doubt, move out of the way. It's better to be embarrassed than squished.

They can't hit you if you're not there applies to pulling off onto the shoulder of the road. When you must stop on the highway, freeway or turnpike, get off, really get off the road. You are going to be a sitting duck so help your odds by getting way off the road.

Bottom Line

Identify potential danger, blind spots and erratic drivers and stay away from them. If you simply cannot avoid riding near these high risk areas, do it with a heightened awareness and do it as quickly (get it over with) as you can. My point is that you can do a lot to keep you and your bike out of harms way.

Riding In the Rain

When it starts raining on your ride, three things happen;

a)   Tires will have less traction
b)   Vision is impaired
c)   You will get wet

All three of these things are going to happen no matter what you do so your option is to either hide out in a coffee shop, or under an overpass, until it stops raining or just deal with it. My personal rain policy is that if I have a choice, I will not ride in the rain but when I have to, I do. In practical terms, if it is raining when it is time for me to go to work in the morning, I will take the car. If the forecast for the day predicts more than a 50% chance of rain, I will take the car. Otherwise, when it rains, I ride in the rain.

Tires Will Have Less Traction

I am purposely avoiding the use of the word slippery here. I don't want you to get all freaked out about the rain and slippery sounds like you are doomed. Actually, riding in the rain can be just another part of everyday riding if you go about it in a safe and sane manner. Don't underestimate the impact of the rain. The laws of physics are not going to change just for you. When a road surface has water on it, your tires will have less traction. You know this from driving a car, but in a car, when you go too fast on wet roads and start sliding or hydroplaning, you have a different result than on a motorcycle.

When it starts raining, common sense tells you to slow down. Never outride your abilities and that includes the abilities of your bike. This does not mean to slow down to a crawl. Can you imagine motorcycle riders in cities like Seattle or London, all slowing down to a crawl whenever it starts to rain? The roads would be paralyzed. Riders who constantly ride in wet weather localities become very accustomed to riding in bad weather and they do so all of the time.

If this is the first rain in the last few weeks, there is the additional problem of road oil and grease floating to the top of the water and causing you to lose even more traction. After a few rains, this problem is minimized by the rain washing this stuff away but it never all goes away. This road oil and grease accumulates on the road and some parts of the road surface have more oil than other parts of the road surface. The lowest concentration is in the car tire tracks. Two tire tracks per lane and they are easy to see during the rain as the cars are constantly running in these tire tracks and "pushing" the rain water to the side. The area between the car tire tracks in the center of the lane has the highest concentration of oil. Next concentration of oil is the area between the lanes themselves. During the rain, try to stay in these tire tracks for the best traction.

The next thing to really watch out for is the traffic paint on the road. You tend not to notice this stuff during dry weather but when it is wet, pay attention. Those 4 foot "STOP" signs painted on the road, the arrows, and the crosswalk outlines are very slick in the rain. That does not mean you must weave in and out to avoid touching any possible paint (Step on a crack and break your mothers back) but do adjust your stopping distance, your turning angle and speed to allow for this "loss of traction" problem.

I had my Sportster for about two months when I got caught in my first rainstorm. I came out of work in the afternoon and it was pouring down. I had leathers and a full face helmet and it had been over forty years since I rode in the rain. This was going to be interesting. I had a twenty mile ride ahead of me, 10 miles on the freeway, and the sky looked like it would get worst before it got better.

There was a huge parking lot where I worked that was about one third full of parked cars. I decided that I need to get some rain riding experience and I need it right now. I rode through the parking lot past the parked cars, got up to about fifty mph, straight line; teeth clenched, and hit the brakes with about 70% of a very hard stop. I was ready to go down. I had my knees clamped tight against the gas tank so I could throw my body weight into controlling the anticipated fishtail.

I was pleasantly surprise that I came to a very quick stop, never lost traction, never fishtailed, I just stopped. Whew, let's try it again. And I did try it again, several more times until I had a crowd of smokers standing outside of the building enjoying the show.

Not every stop was as elegant as the first, but I quickly learned what a good maneuver was and what a bad maneuver was.

Good Maneuvers
a) Slow down dropping down 15% to 20% of your normal speed. Do not become a road hazard yourself but adjust your speed to the conditions.
b) Stop in a straight line, even if the road curves, straighten up your line to stop.

c)   Evenly apply both brakes, don't rely on the rear only or on the front only, keep them evenly applied to avoid losing some control.

d)   Avoid standing water. I know this sounds pretty basic and I do not mean to salomé around each puddle, if you have a choice, avoid standing water.

e)   Ride in the car tire tracks.

Bad Maneuvers

a)   Just the opposite of the good maneuvers above.

b)   Any sudden or jerky move, do everything gradually with plenty of time.

c)   Riding too rigid, too tense, worried about the rain. Relax and get into your normal riding mode. Being on edge, white knuckling the handlebars and being all freaked out is only going to make things worst. The more you ride in the rain, the more confident you will become. Force yourself to relax (easier said than done)

d)   Don't be overconfident. No matter how successful you are the laws of physics still apply to your bike; drop your speed and your cornering angles. For me, I compare riding in the rain with riding on loose gravel. After riding a while in loose gravel (on a dirt bike) you get confident and when you least expect it, it gets you.

Cars Are Not Your Friends

After you have adjusted your speed down to compensate for the rain, riding conservatively and all of that, here's the big problem. As usual, it's the cars on the road with you. As you know, cars are your biggest danger during dry weather and it increased during wet weather.

a)   As they pass you, they will throw a waterfall on you. Getting wet is not the problem, its traction and loss of visibility.
b)   They have the same foggy window problems that you have with your face shield but unlike you, they lose their road and driving focus while they are getting their windows un-fogged. Watch out.
c)   A lot of cars keep the same speed and do not slow down for the weather. It seems like SUV's go faster, challenging the road to test out their four-wheel drive capabilities. I don't get it but I just try to stay away from them.

Vision Is Impaired

Face shield, goggles or glasses all get rained on. Once they get covered with rain drops, not only does your vision drop down to about 35% of normal, but the oncoming car headlights (usually on when it's raining) will turn every drop of water into a miniature light source. This is not good.

Here's what you do. First of all treat your vision protection with anti-fog and rain treatments. The anti-fog treatments will keep the inside of your visor clear (generally) and the rain treatment tends to make the rain run down the outside faster than it would on normal or dirty visors. This is a little bit of help.

CAUTION: Polycarbonates are susceptible to being ruined by using chemicals designed for glass only! Read the label before you apply any chemical to your face shield or other vision protection. You have been warned!

Even with these treatments in place, you will still have rain accumulation on the outside of your glasses or visor. So back to basics, a quick snap of you head will toss the rain off and give you ten seconds of improved visibility.

Windshields may help or hinder the visibility problem. If your windshield is higher than your eye sight line, you will be looking through a zillion miniature light sources and probably still be getting rain directly on your visor or glasses. This is the time that you will be wishing your windshield was lower than your line of sight so you could easily see over it. A lot of riders set their windshield height right at their line of sight so that in dry weather, they can relax and look through the windshield (less buffering) and in wet weather, they can sit erect and look over the windshield.

Tips;

- If you are snapping your head to shake the rain off your glasses, be careful that you don't just flip your glasses off along with the rain.
- Test out your new anti-for and rain treatments on an old visor first. Make sure everything is compatible before you ruin your favorite visor. If the anti-fog treatment doesn't work very well, try another brand. You will eventually find the one that works for you. Then the challenge is to remember during dry weather to routinely apply this stuff so it's in place when you need it.
- Wiping your visor with gloves is OK as long as you do not have some kind of "Terminator" studs and other stuff that will scratch your visor.
- If your impaired vision becomes a hazard, pull of the road and don't get back on the road until the problem

is resolved. Resolved means that you have applied some more rain treatment, switched over to goggles, or it has stopped raining. Taking an unnecessary risk is just not worth the consequences. Just deal with it and be late to whatever appointment you may have. What's more important?

You Will Get Wet

Well that's not too hard to figure out. Every part of your body that is directly exposed to the wind is going to get wet. Your face, chest arms, hands and from you knees down, you are really going to get wet. Plus there are some annoying side effects like water running down your collar, or up your sleeves. Getting wet is just that, getting wet. The big news is losing your focus. All of this wet stuff is very distracting when you really need 100% of your focus on the road surface and all of those cars in the rain out to get you. And unless, you are in a rainstorm in Hawaii or Puerto Rico, you will be getting cold at the same time. Wearing protective weatherproof gear is not so much to keep dry as it to keep you focused on the important stuff as opposed to worrying about that water which is creeping up your sleeve.

> I rode to lunch one day in Reno and ate in a casino. While I was munching on my sandwich and playing the 25¢ Video Poker machine, I heard thunder outside. When I finished my sandwich and headed back to work I was in a torrential downpour. I was wearing Levis, a long sleeved shirt and a vest. No jacket. When I got back to work, about 2 miles away, I was soaked to the bone. That wasn't too bad. The bad part was sitting in front of a computer the rest of the day soaking wet and hating that air-conditioner blowing down on me.

Be Prepared

Those anti-fog and rain treatments which are sitting at home don't do you much good if you need them right now. Your weatherproof riding jacket doesn't do you much good when you don't have it with you. Wearing those low cut loafers may not have been the best choice for today.

So what are you going to do, take everything you need with you at all times? You would be like the traveling "pots and pans" man, a one person motorcycle supply shop on the road. No, but you may consider getting some rain gear and keeping it on the bike during those times of the year when riding in the rain is a real consideration.

Rain Gear

A good riding jacket will weather most of the short duration stuff. Not a 400 mile solution but good enough for a relatively short commute. A rain coat and rain pants are perfect for that rain emergency.

Tips

- Some riders like the golfing style rain gear. Its relatively cheap, rolls up tight to fit in your rack bag and does a pretty good job of keeping you dry. The downside is that most golfers don't have exhaust pipes and if you just touch this polyester plastic to your exhaust you are going to get an instant hole in your rain suit and a lot of elbow grease to get the melted plastic off your exhaust pipe.
- Getting a rain coat or jacket only leaves your pants open to the rain and believe me, from your knees down, you are going to get wet, really wet. So get the pants too. If you wear chaps, they will work except for the crotch which will get wet.

- Get it big enough to go over your riding jacket. Try it on in the store and make sure that it is big and loose enough so it does not restrict you arm movement and so on. The same with the pants, they must pull on over your boots. You do not want to end up dressing and undressing under an overpass just to get your rain gear on. However, if you do that, the rain will usually stop about five minutes after you are all suited up.
- Make sure your rain coat has drawstrings or Velcro to seal up the end of your arms. You do not want water creeping up your arms while you are riding.
- If you get stuck in the rain without your gear and the forecast does not look good, find a local Wal-Mart or Dollar store and get some cheap throw-away rain gear to get you through the storm. Ponchos are not such a good idea, flapping all over the place unless you wrap your belt around the outside and like the samurai look.
- Don't forget about your helmet hanging upside down on the handle bars while you are waiting out the storm in some coffee shop.

Bottom Line

Don't be all freaked out about riding in the rain, just be cautious and use good old common sense. Getting wet never killed anybody but out-riding your ability or losing your focus can be a bad thing. What I like best about riding in the rain is coming up to a red light and stopping next to another wet soul on a motorcycle. Usually there is none of the standard chitchat, just a look of "I feel your pain."

Ahh, that's what it's all about.

What Does It Cost?

Anti-Fog, rain treatment, etc	$20 or less for each
Rain gear	$20 for a throwaway raincoat $50 to $80 for a good MC raincoat $250 for quality MC rain suit

Rules Of The Road

I fired up the Internet search engine and went looking for motorcycle rules of the road. Wow, there seem to be about a zillion "Rules of the Road" and they are always life and death critical. There are rules of the road for staying alive on your motorcycle, about projecting a certain image, riding 2-up (with a passenger), riding in groups, riding in the rain, the heat, rush hour and just about every other situation you might ever encounter in twenty lifetimes. On top of all of this, there are humorous versions that are a lot more fun to read but still are anchored somewhat in motorcycle reality. I don't know about you but for me at least, a zillion is a little over the top for my feeble brain.

Here is my short list, in no particular order, my personal top ten riding rules. These are the rules which I never, ever break.

Table 2. Frank Gates Motorcycle Riding Rules

1	Always wear Helmet, Air-Vest, gloves & boots
2	No alcohol, no drugs while riding, never
3	Always use my turn signals
4	Always look over my shoulder before changing direction
5	Bright beams ON during daylight
6	Always maintain a buffer zone
7	Stay out of car's blind spots
8	No front brake use below 5 mph
9	Always keep it in gear when stopped at a light
10	Never be first away from the stoplight

1) Always wear Helmet, Air-Vest, gloves & boots

I don't even think about it, I just do it. Remember that 50% of all motorcycle deaths are attributed to no helmet.

2) No alcohol, no drugs while riding, never

50% of all motorcycle accidents are alcohol and/or drug related so if you never ride while under the influence, you have just improved your odds by the same 50%.

3) Always use my turn signals

Just make this automatic. Just do it. There is no downside, only improved safety and awareness.

4) Always look over my shoulder before changing direction

I know you just looked in the rear mirror and the lane next to you is clear but look over your shoulder anyway. You may only be surprised in 1 out of a 100 times but that 1 time will be the time you wished you had taken a look. (I wish car drivers would do the same.)

5) Bright beams ON during daylight

Cheap insurance, why not?

6) Always maintain a buffer zone

Not only will this increase your safety level, but keeping a buffer zone around you will keep you focused on your ride. If you are always calculating your buffer zone, you are truly engaged in your ride. You are focused.

7) Stay out of car's blind spots

Redundant, like that country western song about "You never can have too much fun", well you never can have too much rider awareness.

8) No front brake use below 5 mph

Using the front brake at these very low speeds will suck you to the ground like a magnet. If you do get caught in this trap you will be glad you have those boots on.

9) Always keep it in gear when stopped at a light

Evasive action at a stop light means evasive action right now. Always be ready to move out of the way.

10) Never be first away from the stoplight

Not as easy as it sounds. I always want to get out in front (ahead) of the traffic. Intersections are the most dangerous parts of the road. Hang back and let the car(s) on either side of you take the hit from someone who is running the red-light.

I know I missed some of your favorites but if I put in everything, my list would be the top twenty, thirty or fifty rules.

For example: I do check my tire pressure but not every time I get on the bike. When I am riding, I really can feel it when the tire pressure is two or three pounds below normal. You will feel the same thing after you get used to your bike. When it starts to feel mushy or maybe too stiff, I dig out the tire pressure gauge (which I do keep in my tool bag). Otherwise, I will periodically check tire pressure before I ride. At the same time I check all of the bolts, oil and so on. I do this about once a week when I am riding everyday.

Keeping focused, being alert at intersections, keeping my speed within my sight distance are fundamental skills and to me, don't fit on my list, they fit in my brain and they are always ON as an aspect of simply driving the machine.

Just because something is not on the list doesn't mean I don't pay attention to it but if it is on the list, I always do it.

Do I really, really, always obey my list of rules? You betcha! How? Well, you just make a commitment and then just do it.

The definition of commitment: When you sit down to eat a breakfast of ham and eggs, the chicken has made a contribution but the pig has made a commitment.

For me I just put the decision process behind me. When I change lanes, I hit the turn signal. I don't revisit the decision to use turn signals each time I change lanes. I have already made that decision and I just always use the turn signals.

In a car, I do not make a new decision every time on wearing a seatbelt, I just do it. After a while, it really does become pretty much automatic.

They say it takes 21 days to break a habit or to instill a new habit and I agree with that statement.

For example, wearing a helmet whenever I get on the motorcycle is just like wearing swimming trunks in a public pool. You don't even think about going in the pool naked and likewise, I don't even think about getting on my motorcycle without wearing a helmet.

Bottom Line

Now this is my list, you should make your own list. Maybe it will be the same as mine or maybe not. But if you take the time to think through it, weighing each rule on how important it is to you, you will be way ahead of the game. Just making the list will get you thinking of your riding rules and that is a good thing.

Confused yet? Well don't be, just keep it simple and simply enjoy your ride.

Rider Gear

As a teenager, rider gear was probably the last thing I thought about. Maybe if it was really cold, I would wear a jacket.

Today, I put rider gear way up on top of the list. I rank rider gear as important as the motorcycle condition, riding ability and focus. Good quality rider gear can make a significant difference in your ability to get up and walk away from a crash.

As long as you are mandated by law to wear some of this stuff, why not make it count?

Looking Cool vs. Being Safe Matrix

Some people see the glass half full, others see it half empty, and an engineer sees a container that has twice the required capacity.

So what happens when you send an engineer (like me) out to buy riding gear? Well, a matrix, of course.

But what is this matrix? What do I do with it? Well, I believe that when you gear up to go riding, you should make a conscious risk decision. You should understand that there is risk involved in your equipment choices. You should not gear up using a helmet just because your brother had one that sort of fits or a leather jacket that is built for the disco, not for the road. If you are going to wear protective equipment, choose quality gear that will do its job. By reviewing this matrix, you can weigh the gear against the risk. You can get a general idea of what looking cool costs against using gear which may provide a higher degree of protection.

So, for something entirely new and refreshing, I present to you the Frank Gates Cool/Safe Matrix.

Table 3. COOL/SAFE Matrix

	→	→	→	→	→SAFE
	COOL←	←	←	←	←
HEAD Helmet	None	Novelty	Half	Three Qtr	Full Face
EYES Protection	None	Sunglasses	Visor	Goggles	RX
BODY Leather	None	Vest	Jacket	Armor	Air-Vest
HANDS Gloves	None	No Fingers	Light	Heavy	Armor
LEGS Protection	Shorts	Levis	Chaps	Ride Pants	RideSuit
FEET Footgear	Low cut	Cowboy	Engineer	Hiking	Riding

Half **COOL**
Half **SAFE**

On the left side is the totally cool rider, wild hair blowing in the wind, comfortable shorts and a muscle T-shirt. Just the guy you warned your daughter to stay away from. Being totally cool has its risk. Even Arnold wore a leather jacket as the Terminator roaring along on his Fat Boy.

On the right is the maxed out, head to toe, protected rider. Looks like he just got off the race track and he is probably on a sport bike. This rider gets top ratings in the safe department, but seriously lacking in the cool department.

Myself, I choose to be somewhere in the middle, relatively protected and some pretense of being cool.

Where do you fit in?

I should point out that my definition of cool is probably different from your definition of cool. Everybody has their own style and being an individual is what riding is all about.

Here's a brief summary of each of the different categories. The correct gear is very important and there are a lot of considerations besides what looks cool. Each of these is covered in its own chapter later on in the book.

Helmet

To wear it or not to wear it, that is the question. And the answer is pretty easy, if you live in a state that requires you to wear a helmet, that's your answer. If not, then it's up to you. Personally, I will always wear a helmet. It's the smart thing to do.

On the matrix, "none" and "novelty' should be combined as a novelty helmet offers as much protection as no helmet. They look cool, and sometimes fool the police into thinking you have a DOT approved lid on you head. Sometimes, they don't fool anyone. Enough said about novelty helmets.

The remaining three are pretty self explanatory, the more helmet that you have wrapped around your precious head, the less damage you will experience when that same precious head is getting up close and personal with the pavement.

I probably should have put a "flip-up" full face in the list but in terms of safe vs. cool, it's really the same as a fixed full face. Riding with the shield flipped up will put you way off the cool index.

Eye Protection

Eye protection is required in every state and there's no fooling the local sheriff about this one. You either have eye protection or you don't. Sunglasses are universally cool. If you wear prescription lenses, there are a whole different set if issues. A visor helps out with prescription lenses as you can wear your regular glasses behind the visor. I wear prescription lenses and this topic is near and dear to me. Goggles not only will accommodate your regular lenses but are pretty good in the rain. And finally, I put RX Glasses (meaning shatterproof) as the safest.

Leather Jacket

I always wear my leather jacket unless it's up in the nineties. I wondered about this a lot and one day I asked a motorcycle cop who was watching cars reluctantly come to a complete stop (after seeing him) at a four way intersection. I told him that sometimes it was so hot in the jacket that sweat was running down my back. He said that you need to weigh the reality of heat stress against the safety provided by wearing the jacket. If the heat makes you pass out, you are going to go down and it's good to have leather on but if you were not wearing the jacket in the first place, the heat probably would not have caused you to go down. You make the call.

Air-Vest

And then there is the Air-Vest. I wear it all of the time with or without my jacket. Never heard of an Air-vest? It has an internal network of inflatable rubber bags that inflate when you crash. What happens is that the vest is attached to your bike, via steel lanyard, and when you go flying away from the bike, the lanyard pulls the stop out of a CO_2 cartridge and the vest inflates.

Check it out at
http://www.hit-air.com/english/main.html.

Gloves

I like wearing light gloves all of the time. Every time I have gone down (which have not been many), my gloves have saved my hands from abrasion. Winter gloves are big and bulky but when the weather calls for them, they do their job.

Long Pants

Long pants, that's it, no discussion. I wear Levis all of the time. I add chaps when it gets cold. They are a pain, but in terms of safety and weather they are just what the doctor ordered. And unlike most safe gear, they look pretty cool.

Boots

And finally, what goes on your feet. I wear engineer boots and sometimes cowboy boots. I have to be careful with my cowboy boots as sometimes when you put your feet down at a red light, road gravel will lose your footing, real quick. My engineer boots have treads which takes care of this problem.

Helmets

To wear it or not to wear it, that is the question. And the answer is pretty easy, if you live in a state that requires you to wear a helmet, that's your answer. If not, then it's up to you. Personally, I will always wear a helmet. I think it's the smart thing to do.

Three Styles of Helmet

The maximum safety helmet is the full face helmet. Next is the three quarter helmet (lose the face part) and finally, there is the half helmet (lose everything below the eyebrows. All of these have very distinct advantages and disadvantages.

Figure 16 Full Face

Figure 17 Three Quarter

Figure 18 Half Helmet

Novelty Helmet

Let's get this one out of the way right off the bat. To me, the novelty helmet or Beanie is something you wear when you hate wearing helmets but you hate getting pulled over by the police even more. If you are after the Cool Factor (which is very high with these helmets) be aware that there are small profile half helmets out there which are DOT approved and not very much bigger than a typical novelty helmet or Beanie.

On the matrix, "none" and "novelty' should be combined as a novelty helmet offers as much protection as no helmet. They look cool, and sometimes fool the police into thinking you have a DOT approved lid on you head. Sometimes, they don't fool anyone. Enough said about novelty helmets.

Full Face Helmet

[Full Face Helmet]   This helmet has it all. It has a sturdy jaw protector that extends out from your face and effectively protects you entire face from exposure to the asphalt. Most of these full face helmets complete the jaw extension with a protective face shield which covers the entire face "hole". This face shield usually flips up out of your face when you need some air.

If you started riding on dirt bikes or sports bikes, this is the helmet that you are accustomed to wearing.

Safety wise, this is the helmet. Statistically, the more helmet, the less damage you will experience when you hit the pavement.

Road and wind noise wise, this is the helmet. Because your ears are inside, the only wind or road noise is coming up from under the face and through the neck hole. This is a big deal on a long road trip.

While these helmets usually have air vents, they are going to get hot in the hot weather.

Improved gas mileage: Yes, that's right, a full face helmet offers less wind resistance and therefore improves gas mileage.

Also in the cold weather, the full face helmet will surpass all of the others in keeping you warm.

The full face helmet is great with prescription glasses.

Communication is best with this helmet as the wind noise is low for the microphone. This means fewer false keying of the microphone due to ambient noise.

"Get this thing off my head" may be your response to wearing the full face helmet. Everything that makes it great is also what makes it horrible. It is very restrictive in movement. Full face fans will say no way but I think that it is more difficult to look over your shoulder, more difficult just to keep that constant back and forth visual awareness to your surroundings that is critical to safe riding.

It will fog up on you, especially during the rain. There are de-fogging products and as long as you are vigilant about applying them, no problem. But I always seem to remember when the face shield is starting to fog up, not before.

It will rarely fit into your saddlebags.

It really is a large helmet. In fact, some would say, "It is huge!"

Full Face Flip up Helmet

[Full Face Flip up Helmet]   This is the same full face helmet but with the jaw section hinged (like your real jaw is hinged), so that it can be flipped up to the top of the helmet. I like this style and that is what I have. I don't like putting on a non-flip up full face helmet. I feel claustrophobic sticking my head inside, but with a flip up I flip the face up and put on the helmet. Then I flip the face down and everything feels right. Weird, maybe, but that's me.

Three Quarter Helmet

[Three Quarter Helmet]   This is what you usually see motorcycle cops wearing. The three quarter (3/4) helmet offers protection for your whole head except the lower part of your face. It will keep your ears warm in the cold weather and maybe too hot in the hot weather.

Good for communications as you can put speakers and a boom mike in the helmet. Helmet speakers eliminate using earplugs.

Hearing and vision are somewhat affected with this helmet. The hearing is simply muted due to the ear protection. Different manufacturers have different degrees of hearing capability. The vision issue is on the side of the helmet. Put it on and look over your shoulder. Because the helmet sticks out from the side of your head, it is more difficult to see around to the side. Different manufacturers have different styles with some being cut back more than others. The more it is cut back, the easier it is to see but the less area is protected.

This helmet is too big to fit in a lot of the saddlebags out there. Unless you have some saddlebags large enough to accommodate this helmet, you will be leaving it unattended, using a helmet lock or carrying it with you where ever you go.

You can get a face shield with this style of helmet. Most are a flip up face shield style that is usually ratcheted so it will stay in whatever position you lift it into. Manufacturers say you should never ride with the shield up but I see a lot of riders doing just that.

If you wear prescription glasses, this face shield is very handy.

The face shield can protect you from road rocks, bugs and so on and you can get different degrees of tint. I personally think that a clear shield is great. I do not want a tinted shield at night nor do I want to be changing shields while I am on the road. A three quarter (3/4) helmet with a face shield is a pretty good deal to me.

Half helmet

Half helmets are light and unrestrictive. This is a summertime helmet, surface street helmet (low speed), all around use (low and some high speed), offers relatively good protection and pretty cool looking. You can get a visor (built on to the helmet or attached with three snaps) and you can get a face shield. The face shield covers about 1/2 of your face and uses the three snaps for the visor to attach.

My favorite helmet has the face shield built into the helmet itself. It flips up inside of the helmet shell and flips down when you need it.

Figure 19 Visor
UP

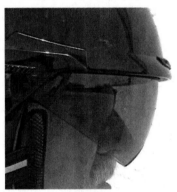

Figure 20 Visor
DOWN

With a half helmet you can hear everything around you, just like you are wearing no helmet. To me this is a good thing. You do want to hear what is going on around you. You want to hear your own bike and how it is running. You want to hear traffic, emergency sirens and so on. You will get wind noise and there are a lot of riders who wear earplugs all of the time. They wear the earplugs that dampen the wind noise but let in other sounds.

This half helmet has great visibility, just as good as no helmet. This again, is a good thing. You always need to look over your shoulder when changing lanes or pulling out into traffic and with a half helmet, you can do so without extra bending and gyrations.

In an accident, the lower half of your head and face is exposed. Road rocks, gravel and bugs are still having their way with your face.

When you are getting up to speed around 60 mph, some half helmets (most of them) will start to aerodynamically lift off the top of your head. You need to keep the chin strap on pretty good. Usually one finger width between the strap and your chin will get it done. At speed, if the helmet starts to rise, you can open you mouth, lowering your jaw into the strap and it will pull the helmet back down. (Watch for bugs while you have your mouth open, flies don't taste too bad but bees just plain suck!)

Communications (needing a microphone) is pretty tough with a half helmet. There are some manufacturers out there that supply boom mikes that will fit onto a half helmet but usually you need a three quarter (3/4) to start getting into the communications game. Of course any music earplugs will work great just remember that there are state by state laws about riding with earplugs and you need to check with you own state to find out what applies to you.

Helmet Color

I read a message from someone on a motorcycle board that said wearing a white helmet will reduce your chances of an accident by 25%. Wow, that's a big number, 25%. Is it true?

But I think that there's more to this particular color issue than just color. I am talking about the unconscious or at least the sub-conscious drivers built in "cop alert" mechanism. I think most drivers are always on some level of consciousness, on the lookout for police. I remember my dad telling me as part of my own driver's education, keep one eye in front of you, one eye on the mirror and your third eye looking for cops.

How to choose a helmet

The ideal is to be in a shop where all of the helmets are available and you can actually try them on. But remember, even after it feels good standing in the showroom, it may not feel so good after riding for two or three hours.

You will probably notice that one manufacturer's line of helmets feels better than another's. Forget about the price or style here. I am saying that one manufacturer has decided to make a helmet that more closely matches your head than the next manufacturer.

When my wife and I picked up our new Harley, we choose HD's full face helmets. Who actually made them, I don't know. They had the HD logo and we paid a lot of money ($235 each). They were cool (still are) with flip up face shield and flip up jaw bar. In fact, it was hard to figure out what flipped up and what stayed still.

The sales clerk, associate, told us that we should select sizes that felt pretty tight as the helmet would loosed up later. We did and now three years and about 18,000 miles later, my wife still calls us Chip and Dale because out faces are so "scrunched" up that we look like a couple of chipmunks peeking out of the helmet. We wear these still whenever we are going for a high speed (freeway) run, even in the hottest weather. They just feel safe.

But the too tight business was some bad advice. Too loose and too tight are both problems. And of course, they are problems that you don't really understand until after you have paid your money and have walked out the door. Yes, I am saying that the helmet needs to fit perfectly. Not too loose and not too tight. Wait, don't give up yet, there are a lot of different helmets out there and they all come in many different sizes.

If you can get to a motorcycle "Superstore" that has literally dozens and dozens of helmets, you are close to success. Even if you have to drive a couple of 100 miles to this store it is worth the trip.

For me, a Medium or Medium plus is about the right size. One manufacturer's medium is another manufacturer's small and a third manufacturer's large. Keep trying until one feels right. You will know it when it feels right.

Too big is when you can snap your head from side to side like you are emphatically saying no and the helmet stays stationary. Your head is literally spinning inside of the helmet. Too small doesn't necessarily mean that you have difficulty getting it on your head, some three quarter (3/4) and full face helmets are difficult to get on but still are the right size. So get it on your head before deciding that it is too small.

With it on your head does it just feel too tight all over like a shrinking rubber glove? If so it is probably too tight. If it feels snug all around but not pressing in on you, you are close to a good fit.

If it all fits wonderfully except a small area on the forehead, put it back. That one little pressure spot will end up being a huge red forehead (your huge red forehead) after a couple of hours of riding. Remember, when you are riding, there is vibration and wind buffering you all of the time and just like a new shoe, you will discover where it really does not fit. The helmets exterior size is right but the interior shape does not fit you head.

Now you have found your size. Armed with the manufacturer, model number and size, you can shop on the internet and probably save some money. Just don't forget that internet shopping adds postage and handling and ten to twelve days of time to the purchase. Then if you get it and for some reason it doesn't fit, you have the return postage and return time to hassle with. Over the internet you can get the color and style you want

If the helmet you like (from the Internet only) has never actually been on you head, here's the deal. Typically, there is a sizing chart that tells you how to measure your head and then convert that measurement into the manufacturer's helmet size. That's great but not all manufacturer's helmet sizes are the same. They sound the same, small, medium and large but they may have different inch or centimeter sizes relating to the small, medium and large designations. So one guy's large may be another guy's medium and so on. You may be returning it for a different size (shipping cost).

Bottom Line

You have many choices of personal protection riding gear. Understand the risk factor for each choice, understand the risk factor for your cumulative choices and then enjoy the ride.

What Does It Cost?

Full Face Helmet DOT	$120 and up
Full Face Helmet w/Flip Up DOT	$120 and up
Three Quarter Helmet DOT	$85 and up
Half Helmet DOT	$85 and up
Novelty Helmet Non-DOT	You are on your own here

Resources

Shoei	Helmet manufacturer	shoei-helmets.com
HJC	Helmet manufacturer	hjchelmets.com
Scorpion	Helmet manufacturer	scorpionusa.com
Nolan	Helmet manufacturer	nolanhelmets.com
Bell	Helmet manufacturer	bellsports.com
KBC	Helmet manufacturer	kbc-helmet.com
Vega	Helmet manufacturer	vegahelmet.com

Eyes

ZZ Top sums it up, "And the choice is up to you cause they come in two classes: Rhinestone shades or cheap sunglasses". No matter if it's a pair of cheap sunglasses, Ray-Bans or some Prada Rhinestones, you will enjoy your ride a lot more without all the tears and blurred vision from the wind in your eyes.

Flying Objects

Yes, literally, flying objects which include every sort of flying bug, stinging sand flying off the top of the cement truck, rocks, bolts, road kill and anything else that you really don't want hitting you in the eyes. You have not really lived until you have blasted through a swarm of bees. Ouch!

Eye protection will not only keep all of this flying stuff from injuring your eyes, but it will avoid these brief moments of high speed panic when something has hit you and blinded one eye. Riding with one painful eye closed, one surviving eye open, while you try to change lanes across the freeway to the shoulder so you can stop and rub it, is a challenge.

Wind and Dust

To me, it is just too risky to try and ride safely with the wind constantly hammering your eyeballs. Tears start running, incessant blinking; this just takes away your focus and makes every move dangerous. Add some dust to the wind and you are blinded.

Rain

The bad thing about wearing eye protection when it is raining is that all of the raindrops hang on your lenses, turning into miniature light sources. They catch oncoming headlights (and now most states have wiper/headlight laws) and reflect those headlights into your vision. The good thing about eye protection when it is raining is that a quick snap of your head is like a quick windshield wiper, flipping off all of the raindrops and giving you a fresh start. Of course, you almost immediately have to repeat it to keep your vision clear. Personally, I would rather have eye protection in the rain than do without.

Sunshade

If your eye protection choice has a dark tint, then you are really improving your vision when riding into the sun. If they also have ultra-violet protection, your eyes will last a lot longer before fatigue gets them.

Wearing tinted eye protection at night is probably not going to help anything. In fact, it's probably not a very good idea at all.

What Types of Eye protection are Out There?

Anything is 100% better than nothing when it comes to eye protection. However, I do not agree with ZZ Tops cheap sunglasses for riding.

> I talked to a local motorcycle cop one day about what did he wear for eye protection. Who would know more than a motorcycle cop who spends 8 hours a day riding on the streets and highways? He said he prefers Ray-Bans. They are strong (won't easily break) and the lenses are unbreakable and have ultraviolet protection. What model? Whatever floats your boat. He even told me where I could get the best deal in town on a pair of Ray-Bans. That's my scientific survey, one cop, and one opinion.

I will tell you that the style of sunglasses plays a significant role in cutting down the wind. The closer they are contoured to fit your eyeball socket, the less wind. That seems pretty obvious. For the same reason, bigger is usually better. There is no substitute for a ride test. What may look cool and just right in the store may turn out to be a loser when you ride. It would be nice if the store owners would let you take them out for a test ride but that isn't going to happen. It's all trial and error, my friend.

Think about buying a backup pair for those times when you leave them sitting on the restaurant table and they are gone when you return.

Motorcycle Glasses

The next step up is to get some motorcycle glasses. This is, of course, a step up in price along with the improved performance. There are several manufacturers of quality motorcycle glasses and I have listed some of these at the end of this chapter in the links section.

Motorcycle glasses are made with motorcycle riding in mind. They are tapered to snugly fit your face around your eyes. Some have thin (1/4 in) foam liners on the outer edge to seal up the face to the glasses. I have had a couple of pairs of these made by Panoptx. I like them. Once you have them on, the foam is not noticeable and they really do cut down on the wind. Because they seal the glasses against your face, sometimes there is a fog problem. There are a number of anti-fog wipes on the market. Just make sure they say they are made for glass. I usually get about two years out of them before the foam starts falling off. I have just torn it off and continued to use them without the foam for another couple of years. No problem, at first I could feel the increase in wind but after a few miles, they felt fine. If you are still within the guarantee, you can send them back to have the foam replaced. The warranty changes with the vendor so check before you buy.

Remember, there are a lot of different face shapes out there and a lot of different styles of motorcycle glasses trying to fit those shapes. Try them on and wear them around the shop to get a good feel for the fit.

Goggles

OK, we are getting into the heavy duty eye protection department here. Look at all of those old timer rider photos from the first half of the last century and you will see goggles everywhere.

Why would you wear goggles? Well, there are a lot of reasons. For one thing, you can put the goggles on your helmet and leave them there when you are not riding. When you go for a ride, put your helmet on and pull down your goggles. Leave the strap around the base of the helmet. It's like having a helmet with a visor. Some helmets have a "belt loop" permanently affixed to the rear to keep your goggles strap from sliding off the helmet. You have not lived until you have your strap slip off the helmet at 70 mph. Whew!

Another reason people use goggles is for the rain. The goggles keep your eye area relatively dry and on a long ride, every little bit of comfort helps.

And some riders wear goggles because they think they look cool. Actually, I think they look pretty cool also.

Goggles Over Glasses

I have a pair of goggles because I normally wear prescription glasses all of the time, motorcycle ride or not. My goggles fit over my normal prescription glasses and to someone who needs prescription glasses, that's a big deal.

Not all goggles will fit over glasses. Make sure that they say they are made to be worn over glasses. There are size restrictions for your glasses and they vary from model to model. The goggle specifications will tell you the height of the glasses which will fit into the goggles. Try them out if possible before you purchase them. When you get a pair of goggles that comfortable fit over your glasses, you will have the best rider eye protection and the clear vision that your glasses normally provide.

Prescription Lenses

I need to wear glasses. I can find my way around without them but I am so used to seeing everything sharp and in clear focus that I wear them always. This complicates the motorcycle eye protection issue.

When I started riding, I tried using a helmet visor for eye protection while wearing my prescription glasses. With a full face or a 3/4 helmet, the face shield is big enough (covers your whole face) so that wearing my glasses was OK. But as I became more and more experienced I found that I really likes a half helmet (that's another chapter) and the half helmet did not get along with face shields very well. Too short, too goofy looking, snap-on-snap-off, where do I put the shield and so on. And being an engineer, I needed to try out just about every possible combination before I gave up and started looking for motorcycle glasses with prescription lenses.

You can get prescription lenses for just about any pair of glasses including motorcycle glasses. Be prepared for the sticker shock, it's not cheap. I bought my first Panoptx glasses with prescription lenses. Including the eye examination, polarized, prescription lenses with transition (auto shades) added, I was close to $500 by the time I put them on my face. For someone who needs to wear glasses, this was one of the best investments I have ever made to ride my motorcycle.

Half helmet freedom, I was totally juiced up about these glasses and six years later, I am just as juiced up as I was then. The downside is (and there's always a downside), now where do I put my regular glasses when I put on my motorcycle glasses? My solution is to always wear a shirt that has a breast pocket. I don't buy T-shirts without pockets. And even with T-shirts that have the pocket, I always wear a jacket or vest that covers the pocket. Without a jacket or vest over the pocket, I have watched my glasses creep up and out of my T-shirt breast pocket in the direct wind. Not good.

What about bifocals? Well, I am glad you asked. I wear bifocals and when I ordered my motorcycle glasses (Panoptx), I elected to skip the bifocal option. I figured that I would not be doing any reading while riding so who cares about bifocals. Well, hindsight is 20/20 and there are some things which I wish I could read better while riding. Like my odometer. I consider my gas gauge to be a real loose estimate of how much gas I have in the tank. When it says I have less than a quarter of a tank left that may mean 40 more miles or 80 more miles. I commute everyday and I have had the experience to know that my mileage is a far more accurate estimate of gas in the tank than the gas gauge. All this really means is that I need to remember to check my odometer (trip-o-meter) when I am stopped at a stop light as I cannot do it when I am moving. I need to lean down a little closer to the odometer to read it and I cannot do that while I am moving.

Another place I miss the bifocals is entering PINs and following text directions at the gas pump. How big of a deal is this? Well, I probably still will not get bifocals with the next new pair of motorcycle glasses. It just is not that big of a deal for me and my vision.

Helmet Visors

Even with all of the variations of helmet visors available, I still wear my motorcycle glasses under the visor. For me it's that prescription thing. I could wear my regular glasses under the visor (and I do occasionally) but I like the motorcycle glasses. If there is any kind of visor problem, I don't have to worry about riding with my regular glasses as my only eye protection. That's just what I do. You may find that the visor is just what you want and that's that. You need to decide what works for you, not me.

Do I Need Eye Protection?

Eye protection is required in every state and there's no fooling the local sheriff about this one. You either have eye protection or you don't.

On a rider level, do you need eye protection? It is similar to the helmet-no-helmet debate that is continuously debated. I think you need eye protection but if I was against it, I am sure I could come up with some sort of semi-convincing argument against eye protection.

Issues/Concerns

I have covered all of the expected stuff but there another loose end.

Where do I put my expensive motorcycle glasses when I leave my bike outside of the cinema for two hours? Remember, these motorcycle glasses are shaped to fit your face and when you fold them up, they do not fold up as flat as regular sunglasses. In fact, they end up being about a fat as a tennis ball. They all come with a cover, usually large enough to hold a tennis ball. Hang them by one of the temples (the part that goes over your ear) in the v-neck of your sweater? Pretty expensive loss if they fall out or off the top of your head? It's easy to lose them.

I put them in my helmet which is hanging upside down from the handlebars. My gloves go in the helmet on top of the glasses. If I do not trust my helmet to still be there when I return, I carry the whole thing with me into the cinema.

Bottom Line

Protect your eyes from road hazards by wearing protective lenses. If you need corrective lenses, (prescription) lenses, buy some high quality motorcycle glasses with your prescription lenses in them.

What Does It Cost?

Motorcycle Glasses	$50 to $175
Motorcycle Glasses, Prescription	$50 to $175 for glasses, add prescription cost from your lab
Goggles	$50 to $150
Goggles over Glasses	$30 to $150
Face Shields	$20 or less, Half Helmet add on

Resources

Bolle	Performance Sportswear: Again, one International Biggie.	www.bolle.com
PanOptx	In the same league with Wiley X, one of the biggies.	www.panoptx.com
Wiley X	Wiley X sunglasses and goggles by Protective Optics was born in 1986 to	www.wileyx.com

	produce ballistic eyewear for U.S. Military Special Forces and Law Enforcement agencies nationwide.	

And there are many more, you may be surprised. Just because I did not list their link here does not in any way diminish their products.

Body

Protective gear for the body (torso) performs three functions. It helps protect you from weather, abrasion and it helps protect you from physical damage such as broken bones. Not all types of protective gear do all three functions. Fore example, a leather jacket without any additional armor built into the jacket, will primarily protect you from the weather and abrasion but not do much to prevent broken bones. There are compromises and risks associated with your choices of body protection.

	➔	➔	➔	➔	➔ SAFE
	COOL ←	←	←	←	←
HEAD *Helmet*	None	Novelty	Half	Three Qtr	Full Face
EYES *Protection*	None	Sunglasses	Visor	Goggles	RX
BODY *Leather*	None	Vest	Jacket	Armor	Air-Vest
HANDS *Gloves*	None	No Fingers	Light	Heavy	Armor
LEGS *Protection*	Shorts	Levis	Chaps	Ride Pants	RideSuit
FEET *Footgear*	Low cut	Cowboy	Engineer	Hiking	Riding

Looking at the Cool/Safe Matrix, I have the coolest looking body protection listed as none. This is the happy rider wearing just a T-shirt and enjoying the ride. Next increase in body protection adds a vest. Not a very big step up towards the safe zone but a little better than just a T-shirt. Then I add a jacket. Leather or nylon (ballistic) are both good and will make a big difference in weather and abrasion protection. Next up I have listed armor. By this I mean armor inserts in the elbows, shoulders and back. You now have the full package of body (torso) protection.

But wait, there's more, there is the Air-Vest. The Air-Vest is just what it sounds like, a vest with a built in air-bag. I wear it all of the time with or without my jacket.

Vests

I think that vests are one of those items that people either love or hate. I am in the love camp. I love my vest(s). Yes, I have more than one. I think the main reason I am so enamored with wearing a vest is all of the pockets where I can stash all of my essentials. Essentials like my glasses, my digital camera, my dog treats (for training my dog), my cell phone, my ear plugs, and those surprise items which end up in my large inside pocket. OK, maybe it is a lot of junk, but I do it and love it all the same.

Figure 21 Vest Front

Figure 22 Vest Inside Pocket

Figure 23 Vest Rear

A vest does not do very much for you in the protection department thought. It is a little warmer in cold weather and a little dryer in wet weather.

Does it look cool or not? Well, that's up to you. A lot of riders like to sew on patches (ride patches, HOG member, etc.) and it really becomes a visual diary of the rider's adventures, tastes and opinions.

Outlaw Motorcycle Club (MC)

One thing I should mention is if you are wearing a vest with some patches on it, be careful not to get it looking too much like a member of an outlaw motorcycle club. Rocker panels on the back and a "MC" patch should be avoided. I know, it's a free country and all of that, I am just suggesting you may want to consider avoiding the outlaw motorcycle club look. I have never had any problems with outlaw clubs but then again, I don't look like I am a member of any club when I am out and about. I have read that there clubs are very territorial and usually, if you pick a fight with one member, you are picking a fight with the entire club. I guess I am a live-and-let-live kind of guy and wearing outlaw club looking patches on my vest is not important enough to me to make it an issue.

Other Vests

There are leather vests, fabric vests, vests made from chains, fur vests, and camouflage vests and so on. Just like everything else, there are good quality vests and poor workmanship vests. I happen to like a zipper in the front as opposed to buttons or snaps to close the vest. You can get button extenders (a short chain) to pull your vest closed over a big stomach. Heavy leather or thin leather is mostly a cosmetic thing as a vest does not play a very important role in protection.

Jacket

You want your jacket to be comfortable, warm in the cold weather and air circulation in the heat. You want it to provide protection from abrasion and armor to avoid unnecessary broken bones. You want it to be highly visible to other motorists. You want it to do it all but as with most things, there is compromise. It is very difficult to do it all.

There are motorcycle jackets and then there are fashion jackets. Get a real motorcycle jacket. A cool looking leather jacket that was made for fashion will not help you out very much when you are skidding along the asphalt. Sometimes, the non-motorcycle jacket is heavy duty and really looks like the real deal. Don't be fooled. You can tell by the actual cut of the jacket.

Motorcycle jackets are cut so that the rear of the jacket hangs down lower than usual. This is so when you are sitting on your bike, the back covers you all the way down over the top of you pants. A non-motorcycle jacket will ride up leaving an inch or two of exposed back. Also, a motorcycle jacket is cut with the sleeves longer than usual. When you are standing, a motorcycle jacket sleeves will hang down low to you fingers, not stop at your wrist. Again, this makes enough sleeve so that when you are riding, your arms are protected all the way up into or over your gloves. These are two sure indicators that the jacket was made for riding not just the disco.

Another thing that I have a preference for is the end of the sleeves, cuff closure technique. A snap that tightens up the sleeve cuffs but leaves the expansion slit hanging open for wind to get in, is not a good thing when it is cold outside. Zippers are the best. It may sound petty but at 65 mph, that small opening in your sleeves will drive you crazy. And, being driven crazy is OK; it is the loss of focus that is the problem. While you are thinking about that chilly wind running up your arms, you may not notice the truck taillight up ahead. Ouch!

Also, the collar is a big deal. I have a police style leather jacket. Like the one Arnold wore in Terminator. The zipper is off-set (you've seen these) so when you zip it all the way up, it does not end in the center of your body, under your neck, but about three inches off to the side. This pulls the opposite side up to your neck, leaving a solid piece of jacket across the front of you neck instead of a scratchy zipper pull. I like that.

When it is really cold, I wear a leather bandana across my lower face, tucked inside of my jacket top. I look like a train robber but that $15 piece of leather makes the huge difference.

I also like mandarin collars (Arlen Ness, Mansfield jacket) with a snap. Not only do they do a good job of keeping the wind out, I think they look pretty cool.

Material

Leather is the most popular material for motorcycle jackets. It is the traditional material and up until a few years ago, it was in another league than textile jackets. Technology has changed that and textile is right up there with leather today. I like both. I like the look of leather, the feel of leather and the pliability or comfort of leather. I like the way leather ages and even looks better and better the older it gets. I wish I was that way.

Textile jackets (Dupont Cordura nylon for example) are now as tough as leather and to some, more desirable. There are numerous kinds of textile jacket materials. Pricewise, the textile jackets can do the same job as leather at a significantly lower price. What the heck does that mean Frank, significantly lower price? Well, it means 40% or 50% lower.

Air Circulation

Air vents are a must have feature. Typically you will find these on each forearm, in top, zipper closure, which allows onrushing air to enter your sleeve and cool down your arms. Chest air vents and back air vents are wonderful when you are really cooking in the sun. Do these vents cool you down like air conditioning? Not hardly. Sometimes the design is such that you can't even get them to stay open. But even when everything is working great, you still have hot air circulating around your body. It's better than no air but it's not a winter wonderland.

Textile jackets have some pros and cons over leather jackets and air circulation is a plus. Both do a good job of preventing abrasion (leather or ballistic nylon) but the textile jacket is a little more versatile in hot weather. You can get a "summer" version that has small perforations in the nylon allowing some air to get in there and cool you off. You can get perforated leather also but I don't like them. I prefer the textile perforations.

Visibility

One of the leading causes of accidents is punctuated by the statement, "I never saw him coming." The more visibility you can offer the other guy's eyes, the better off you are. You can get jackets with hot pink and yellow colors. Or more moderately, bright colored stripes. I think everyone agrees that the brighter colors are the sensible thing to have but everyone seems to think that the other rider needs these colors, not them.

Sewn in reflective strips or piping is great also. Headlights light them up from a long distance away and distinguish your motorcycle taillight from a car taillight by showing the other drivers that there is a person riding on top of that taillight. This is pretty cheap, must have, insurance, I think.

Armor

"In for a penny, in for a pound", someone said. If you are going to spend the cash for a reasonable jacket, why not get the armor in it at the same time. You should have elbow pads, shoulder pads and some back pads. Your body will thank you. This armor will increase the size of your jacket and possible your maneuverability within the jacket but not if you get a well designed jacket. Remember, you are buying a jacket to wear while you are sitting on your bike, maybe for hours at a stretch, not a fashion accessory to wear to the club.

It has to be comfortable because if it is not comfortable you will not wear it.

Air-Vest

Never heard of an Air-vest? This is a controversial item. Check it out and you may decide this is silly or it may be just the thing for you.

| Figure 24 Air-Vest Front Open | Figure 25 Air-Vest Front Closed | Figure 26 Air-Vest Rear |

I wear an air vest every time I ride. No, it's not what you think. It does not have a car air-bag hanging out the back or a life raft wrapped around my neck. It looks like a normal vest. Built inside of this vest is a rubber, inflatable backbone. Inflated it increases the outside diameter of the vest by about 2 inches.

It has an internal network of inflatable rubber bags that inflate when you crash. It has a CO_2 tube zipped up inside what normally would be a vest pocket. This has a quick release plug that hooks onto a lanyard which in turn, hooks onto my motorcycle. In the event that I go flying off the bike, the lanyard pulls the CO_2 plug and the vest inflates within ½ second. It remains inflated for 30 seconds and then it slowly bleeds air out until it is deflated.

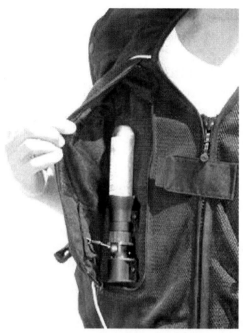
Figure 27 Air-Vest Cartridge

It was not cheap at $500 and I bought one for my wife also. However, I personally think it's a great idea.

I have been wearing it for over one year and thankfully, I have yet to test it out.

Before I bought it, I spoke to a rider (phone call) in Pennsylvania who was wearing an air vest when he went down on the PA Turnpike at 70 mph and walked away from the accident. He was wearing all good safety gear, full face, and full leathers and riding boots. Impressive story, I was sold.

Here are some random bits about air-vests;
- (Humor) If you inadvertently activate the air vest while you have a rider, does the rider get blown off the bike?
- (Humor) If you wear too small of a size air vest, when it inflated does it pop your head off?
- $500 is a lot of money but still less than one ambulance ride.
- Japanese motorcycle police have been wearing air vests for the last ten years.

I figure that it helps prevent broken ribs and such and I am all for that. Because it looks pretty cool and is easy to wear, I am wearing it.

There are several different manufacturers and several different approaches. I heard of one variation that replaces the lanyard with a radio link, no lanyard. This is emerging technology and likely to change rapidly.

Rain Proof

Rainproof jackets are a hard call for me. Leather comes with its own rain proofing built in, so we are talking about non-leather jackets. If rain is a consistent issue with you and where your ride, then certainly, rain proofing makes sense. If rain is a sporadic thing, then maybe a carry along raincoat is the solution. I just think that a good quality jacket should withstand the rain without any additional rain proofing. Of course, where I ride, it is sunny most of the year. Hmmm, maybe that's it, you think?

Odds and Ends

There are some great combination jackets out there also. Zip off the sleeves and you have a vest. Remove the liner (most have this) and you have a summer jacket. Remover the "outer" and you have a summer jacket. Just don't forget that when you are on the road, all of the stuff you remove has to get strapped onto your bike somewhere.

Jacket quality is dependent upon the craftsmanship that went into the jacket when it was manufactured. Stitching that will not tear apart upon impact and material that will stand the direct sun without crystallizing. It must have the flexibility to keep you focused on the road instead of focused on your jacket. This is an area where you really do get what you pay for. I say spend the money to get a top quality jacket and hope you never need to test it out on the asphalt.

Tips

- Some folks take that 6 foot security chain and run it through the sleeves of their jacket to lock the jacket to the bike while shopping or away from the bike.
- Leather face mask for cold weather is the best bargain out there. Less than $20, shaped like a bandana (imagine a cowboy bandit robbing the stagecoach) with Velcro in the back of your neck. This will really make a difference when the temperature drops into the thirties and below.

What Does It Cost?

Jacket, Leather, serious MC jacket	$400
Jacket, Textile	$250
Jacket, Armor	$100 inserts
Vest,	$50 and up
Air Vest (Hit-Air)	$500

Resources

Air-Vest	The "Hit Air" jacket uses CE certified armor to protect the shoulders, elbows and the spine but most importantly, the "Hit Air" jacket also incorporates an air cushion system.	hit-air.com
Arlen Ness	Arlen Ness is a pioneer in the custom motorcycle industry	arlenness.com

There are a ton of sites out there that sell jackets. Everything you can imagine. When you are shopping and you see a $450 leather jacket on sale for $59.99, you really need to ask yourself if this is really possible. Go to your local bike shop and try on a dozen different jackets and get to understand the difference between a quality jacket and a "knock-off."

Find the jacket you like and then go shopping on the internet. Now that you know the model and the size, you can find the best deal.

Hands

Protection is the purpose of wearing gloves. They protect you from those accidental brushes against a hot engine or exhaust pipe, they keep your hands warm in the cold weather and they minimize the road abrasion when you go down.

Correct Fit

You want to get a pair of gloves that fit correctly. If they are too large, you will lose that nice, comfortable feeling of control over the handgrips and controls. Too small and they will always be tighter than necessary and become annoying after even a twenty minute ride. You will know when you put them on if they are a good fit or not. Trust me, you will know.

Two Basic Glove Types

There are basically two kinds of gloves, light weight summer gloves for hot weather and heavier, gauntlet type gloves for cold weather. You can get just about any variation you can imagine, summer gloves with gauntlets, winter gloves without gauntlets, gloves with no fingers, armor, Kevlar, carbon fiber gloves, leather gloves, heated gloves and on and on.

I like leather but right now I am wearing textile gloves. You really need to get your hands into all different kinds at your local MC shop and you will know what you like or dislike.

I am a real stickler for how the Velcro closure straps work. They must be easy to manipulate with a glove on. Presumably, you will always have one glove on when you are closing the Velcro strap on your other glove. Try them out, it they are awkward, move on to another style. Snaps, r=drawstrings and all of the other non-Velcro options just are not my choice, too complicated or too hard to work. Make sure that when you have the gloves on, the Velcro strap has a good fit onto the receiving piece of Velcro. If it only fits halfway on because your hands are the wrong shape for the contour of the glove, then that Velcro will always be coming loose in the wind, at speed. I hate trying to reach across the handlebars to the opposite side to refasten the strap which has come loose and is now sucking wind up my sleeve.

What about reading your watch? Well, any gloves with gauntlets are going to prevent you from reading your watch. But even short summer gloves, which will be presumably covered with your extended motorcycle jacket sleeves, will make doing a one handed peek at your watch pretty hard. Like Peter Fonda said in "Wild Hogs" at the end of the movie, "Lose the watches."

I have two sets of gloves that I wear all of the time (no, not at the same time). I have a light pair without gauntlets for average to warm weather and a heavy pair with gauntlets for cold weather. During the spring and fall, I usually wear my heavy gloves in the mornings and my light gloves in the afternoon, leaving the unused pair in my "Sausage Bag" (What the hell is my Sausage Bag? Well, it's a bag that was sold as a handlebar bag but I use it strapped to the back of my sissy bar, resting on my small luggage rack. It looks short and fat, like a sausage.)

Gel In The palm

If you are riding an older Sportster (pre-2005) or other bike with serious handlebar vibrations, gloves with gel inserts on the palm side of the gloves will really make a positive difference. They cost a little more but for me, the gel gave me an extra hour of riding before the vibrations just wore my hands out.

Bottom Line

I recommend that you make wearing gloves a mandatory safety precaution. Putting on your gloves should become as automatic as putting on your helmet.

I like wearing light gloves all of the time. Every time I have gone down (3 minor falls), my gloves have saved my hands from abrasion. Winter gloves are big and bulky but when the weather calls for them, they do their job.

You can probably tell by now that I love this stuff. What I love the most about gloves is that when I put on my gloves, I know that the next thing I am going to do is to start it up and go. Once the gloves are on, it's time to ride.

Besides all of that, they look cool.

What Does It Cost?

Gloves, summer, leather	$50 and up
Gloves, summer, leather w/GEL inserts	$75 and up
Gloves, summer, textile	$40 and up
Gloves, winter, leather	$50 and up
Gloves, winter, textile	$40 and up

Legs

Anyone who rides a motorcycle while wearing only a pair of shorts is just plain stupid. There, I said it. If you don't like it, well, what can I say? I mean, you are on a hot, heavy machine, doing 50 mph or more, as close to the ground as you can get, and you are going to chance your bare lags against the asphalt? Come on, a little common sense please. And then on top of that I see the same bare legged riders with a passenger who is wearing shorts. I can hardly bear to watch.

Now that I have removed any doubt on where I stand on wearing shorts while riding a motorcycle, let's talk about the real world of riding a motorcycle. Leg protection is a must. No question. You must wear long pants at the very minimum and armored riding pants at the maximum. Let's take a look at your options.

Levis

I wear Levis all of the time. They are my all around choice of pants. I wear them when I am riding to work and I am fortunate that I am allowed to wear them at work. It's easy. But I never forget that Levis offer virtually no protection from abrasion or broken bones.

They are tough, they handle all kinds of weather, they are easy to maintain and they look cool. Sliding across the asphalt at 50 mph will give you about 2 seconds of protection before it is bare skin against the road. Don't fool yourself into thinking that Levis will offer you the kind of protection you really want when you need it.

Wearing Levis is a risk and I accept that risk.

Armor Levis

One step up the scale towards safety is armored Levis. There are pretty cool. There are a few different types out there and basically they have Kevlar armor reinforcement panels in the knees and buttocks areas. They are built to look as unobtrusive as possible and they typically look like a pair of Levis or jeans with heavy knees and backside. There's a video out there showing some guy wearing these Kevlar reinforced Levis while being pulled with a rope attached to the back of a pickup truck. He is sitting on the asphalt and doing about 30 mph on his reinforced butt. No sparks flying but I bet it got pretty warm down there, impressive. They run about $80 a pair and while they are not for me, you should check them out.

Leather Pants

OK, here we go. Leather is going to offer a lot more abrasive protection than Levis. They make leather pants that are cut just like Levis and don't look too bad. They will keep your legs warm or at least out of the wind while riding just like chaps but unlike chaps, they have all of the pockets, belt loops and so on that make them desirable.

Unlike chaps, you usually cannot just put them on or take them off while you are shopping at Wal-Mart. Once you put them on, they usually stay on until the end of the ride or the end of the day. They are hot in the summer but they are a safe option to Levis. It's really all in your taste.

Chaps

I add chaps when it gets cold. They are a pain, but in terms of safety and weather they are just what the doctor ordered. And unlike most safe gear, they look pretty cool.

They are good in cold weather as they stop the wind completely. They are cut long enough so the hang down to about 1/2 inch above the bottom of your heel while riding. With good boots, the lower half of your body is warm and cozy.

Here are some things to look for when shopping for chaps.

- Solid front panels mean they were not pieced together, usually more expensive but it eliminates the cross seams resulting from piece construction.
- The "belt" part is split in the rear and tied together ala shoestring style. Easily adjustable if you are going to lend your chaps to someone else or if your body size expands and contracts a lot. This style of belt adjustments simply allows the manufacturers to make "one size fits all" waist sizes. I like the solid belt with no shoestrings.
- Length should be for riding, not walking. Just like long sleeves on your jacket, chaps need long legs so when you are in a sitting position; they do not ride up to your ankle. Typically, if they touch the ground when you are standing, they are the right length when you are riding.
- Leather thickness is pretty self explanatory. The thicker, the better the protection but the stiffer and heaver the chaps.
- Get an outside pocket on the chaps. It is really handy for your keys. In and out without going through all of the acrobatics required to get into your pockets while wearing your chaps.
- Brass zippers are the hot setup. You really want quality zippers that will not get stuck or are difficult to zip/unzip. If you have ever watched someone taking off

their chaps when a zipper stuck halfway, using one hand, hopping up and down, you will know why quality zippers are necessary.
- Silk or some sort of fabric lining inside the leather is nice as it allows the chaps to go on and off without "sticking" to you pants (Levis).

If you decided to go for some very high quality chaps with all of the bells and whistles, you may want to consider having them custom made for you. You can do all of this online using the vendors measurement sheet and you end up with exactly what you want. Good fit, correct style and so on. Once you up in the $200 or more range, this becomes a viable option.

The downside of chaps is putting them on and taking them off. If you are wearing them every day, you get into a routine and they are just another item of clothing you put on before you go out the door. If you are wearing them on weekends only or only infrequently, you are going to forget you keys in your pocket, put on your chaps and then have a hell of a time getting your keys out of your pocket.

Back to Wal-Mart, where do you put your chaps while you are away from your bike? Well, choice number one is to keep wearing them. Choice number two is to roll them up and put them in your saddlebags or bungi them to your seat. This is a risky choice because a nice roll of leather is a likely target for some passerby to grab and run.

Riding Pants

There are a surprising number of choices of riding pants. Pants that come with a matching jacket (more of a BMW kind of deal), pants made out of leather or textile with suspenders (kind of a bib overall deal) and over pants (slips on over your work Dockers). I include this section just so you are aware of these options.

What Does It Cost?

Levis, Kevlar armored	$110
Chaps, leather	$75 and up, $400 for high quality
Pants, leather	$100 and up (look for discounts)
Pants, riding	$200 and up

Resources

Paul's Harness Shop	Our premium quality motorcycle chaps are American made in our Colorado Springs, CO leather workshop.	phssaddlery.com
Draggin' Jeans	Five times stronger than steel yet soft and pliable, Kevlar® fabric lines the knees and seat of our jeans, providing superior protection where the motorcycle rider most needs it.	dragginjeans.com

Feet

And finally, what goes on your feet is a pair of boots. I see riders wearing tennis shoes everyday and I am always amazed. Penny loafers, slaps and dress shoes just do not have any place in your protective equipment inventory. I have even seen people riding bare foot. I mean, how do you even shift? That must be brutal. So, in my book, boots it is. It is not a question of "if" it is a question or "what type" of boots.

As with all of the other protective gear, your boots must be comfortable. You do not want your focus distracted because your feet hurt. That said there are two main things that you want from a pair of motorcycle boots:

1. Ankle support is important while you are riding for strength and endurance and if you should go down, to protect your ankles. Any boot height lower than your ankles is not the boot you want.
2. The non slip soles help keep your feet on the foot pegs or floorboards. When you stop at a light and put your foot down, you do not want it to go slipping away from you. Any grip in the sole helps stabilize you when you are standing still or walking your bike.

So what kind of boots are you going to get? I wear engineer boots and sometimes cowboy boots. I have to be careful with my cowboy boots as sometimes when you put your feet down at a red light, you will lose your footing, real quick. My engineer boots have treads on the soles which help prevent this problem.

I am absolutely convinced that spending the money for a quality pair of boots is the smart way to go. As a lineman, climbing telephone poles in my early career, I bought a pair of "Wesco" climbing boots. After three years and a couple of thousand poles, they were still in pretty good shape. Good craftsmanship and good materials make the difference. When you are selecting your motorcycle boots, you can choose a low quality boot but I think you will be back buying a second pair a lot sooner that if you had purchased a high quality pair. How do you know low from high quality? This is easy, it's the price.

Rider Boots

These are made specifically for motorcycle touring or racing. These are strictly "on the bike" boots.

Tips

- Get heels tall enough to comfortable hook on the foot pegs but not so tall that they can catch on stuff that you do not want them to catch on.
- Some (high quality) boots have a shifter guard sewn onto the top (above the toe) of the left foot. This is really great as without it, you will see a noticeable wear spot on your left boot after a couple of thousand gear shifts. Required, not hardly, just nice.
- Gore-Tex is a miracle textile, it breathes. It lets the heat go out of your boot and keeps the rain from coming in. This is on hiking boot styles only.
- Are your boots going to be double duty, riding and other uses? Keep this in mind when you are selecting your boots.

Bottom Line

To me there is no question that good boots are always required when riding. I believe that you should never take a chance on riding with anything less protecting your feet.

What Does It Cost?

Harley Davidson Brand MC Boots	$80 to $140 (look for discounts)
Wesco MC Boots	$400 and up, high quality
Double-H Boots	$150 (I wear these)
Alpinestars Tech 10 Boots	$450 and up, touring-racing

Resources

Wesco Boots	After dedicating the last 87 years to making handcrafted boots, we've learned a thing or two.	westcoastshoe.com/wesco
Double-H Boots	It's a passion we experience everyday with western boots and footwear made for your life. Comfortable. Durable. Functional.	doublehboots.com

Motorcycle Gear

Lights

Headlights

Always on

Modern day motorcycles (since mid-1970) are wired so that the low beam headlight is always on when the engine is running. This is a safety issue, having the headlights (and taillights) on during daylight hours helps the other drivers see you. Most states mandate this in the vehicle code (check your local vehicle code).

Daylight Bright Beam

In most states (check your local vehicle code) it is permissible for motorcycles to use the bright beam during daylight hours. I personally think this is a good idea. My unscientific survey (taken as a long time car driver), reveals that a motorcycle coming up behind me on the highway generally remains unnoticed unless they have their bright beam kicked on. With the bright beam on, I usually notice the motorcycle in my rear view mirror early on. The light attracts my attention to my rearview mirror more quickly that my normal driving routine of periodically checking it.

Oncoming motorcycles, even without the headlight on, are no special deal and I see them just as I see oncoming cars. Oncoming motorcycles with the bright beam on catch my eye very quickly as it is annoying. Yes, annoying but you know what, mission accomplished. I see the motorcycle early on and I continue to see the motorcycle until we pass each other and it is behind me.

As a general rule, I leave my bright beam on all of the time during the daylight hours. You must consciously do this by switching it on when you start your ride.

Bright Beam Warnings to others

Annoying is how I described the oncoming motorcycle with the bright beam on and as a car driver, I stand by that statement. It works, you will be noticed. And if you really want to get some car drivers attention, switch your bright beam back and forth to low and hi a few times. You will stand out in the crowd. And you will be legal doing so (check with your local vehicle code).

Here is where this hi-low switching technique really comes in handy. An oncoming car is planning to make a left hand turn (their left hand) across your lane in front of you. This is a leading cause of motorcycle vs. car accidents and it is not unusual for the driver of the car to swear that they never saw you. You can make eye to eye contact and they will still pull out right into you as you try to go pass them. This situation is right up there with intersections as the most dangerous place for a motorcycle to be on the road.

When you see this situation shaping up, start your hi-low switching and really let that driver know you are there. Shake them out of their daydream about their job or relationship and get their focus back on the road. Back on the road that has you on a motorcycle heading for a possible collision if the driver doesn't see you.

Annoying to the driver, I hope so. When I get the driver to return the hi-low flash with the car headlights, mission accomplished. I know I have been seen. If I leave a trail of annoyed left turn drivers behind me every time I ride, so be it. I will take the drivers annoyance over my flying through the air over my handlebars.

Headlight Modulator

This takes the hi-low switching one step further. You can buy a small headlight module that connects to your headlight power wires and will turn your headlight from hi to low all day long. It depends on a daylight sensor to turn this feature off at night plus there is a manual override that gives you the option of turning it on or off anytime (except nighttime).

End result is that your motorcycle will have the headlight switching from bright to low all of the time during daylight hours.

Is this legal? Yes it is legal as long as it complies with the Federal Motor Vehicle Safety Standards (FMVSS 108, 49 CFR Part 571.108 S7.9.4). Generally speaking, if you buy one of these modules from a vendor as opposed to building it yourself, it should be in compliance. Nighttime modulation is not legal in any state.

Have You Seen One Of These Headlight Modulators In Action?

Maybe one of these equipped motorcycles has come up behind you before and caught your attention very fast. I think what catches your eye is the light but what catches your brain is the initial reaction that it must be police or an emergency vehicle. No matter what causes it to get your attention, mission accomplished. Will you annoy a lot of drivers, probably? Will this device save your life, who can say? It really does enhance your ability to be seen by other drivers.

Installation

This is a relatively simple install splicing wires and so on. The module itself goes into your headlight shell (enclosure). Do I have one on my bike? No.

<u>Upgrade lamp</u>

Now this is interesting. One of the riding rules (at lease in my personal rule book) is to not outride your ability. Likewise, do not outride your headlights. What this means is that your headlight has a fixed distance of road visibility or illumination. It is the same distance if you are going 35 mph or 95 mph. The difference is that at 35mph you probably will have time to stop before hitting something which suddenly appears in your headlight like a deer or a ladder on the road. However at 95 mph, you are going too fast to stop in time. You have out ridden your headlights. If you add some fog or rain to the picture, that safe speed drops even more.

One modification is to increase the distance of your headlight illumination. The problem with this is that you still must keep you headlight under control so you stay legal and do not blind any oncoming traffic. This now becomes an issue of quality of light.

In the simplest terms, you just change out your existing headlight bulb for a more powerful headlight bulb. Of course in the real world nothing is ever that simple. Putting in the wrong rated bulb may increase the current draw and heat up your wiring and cause you some significant wiring problems.

<u>How Do I Know What Replacement Bulb To Use?</u>

First of all you need to know about your stock bulb. It will be listed in your owner's manual. Additionally, your headlight lens will have the bulb info molded into it. And finally, the bulb itself will have the type and wattage on its base. A direct replacement with the newer Xenon or Halogen headlight bulbs will give you the additional luminescence. These bulbs have the same ratings as your stock bulb but they use different technology to improve the light quality. If you replace your stock bulb with a bulb that has a higher rating, you are entering the world of heated wires. How much will cause what problems, I don't know. I do know if you are really serious about pumping up your headlight power, you can check the motorcycle forums on the Internet and learn about results other have experienced. You are on you own here.

Add on light bar

I am talking about adding a light bar to compliment your stock, single headlight. This light bar will bring two additional, smaller lights into the game. If you are interested in this, I suggest that you look to your bikes manufacturer and see what they offer. The manufacturer will have developed this add-on light bar specifically for your model of bike and they will have intimate knowledge of increased current draw, mounting issues and so on. If this is not an option, there are numerous after-market vendors out there who sell generic light bars and they will know what fits your specific bike.

A word of caution is warranted here. Although the vendor will supply detailed installation instructions, you are making a serious modification to your bikes electrical system. If this (electronics) is an alien world to you, you may want to consider having your local MC shop do the installation. If you get caught riding at night and your headlight fails, you are through riding at least for that night until you get it fixed. No problem if you are at the corner store, big problem if you are halfway between Reno and Las Vegas.

Taillights

Tail Light & Brake Light Modulator

You can modify your tail light so that it is always blinking. The theory is that more people will see this and that enhances your visibility. There are many variations of this modification. I did read somewhere that the alternative school of thought is that drivers will be attracted to the pulsating taillight (like moths to a flame) and instead of staying away from you, they will get closer and closer. Fact or fiction, you be the judge.

These modifications will cause your brake light to do some attention grabbing stuff.

One approach is a deceleration module. When you hit the brake, the taillight will pulse rapidly, slowing to a solid brake light after three or four seconds. The car behind you may (or may not) understand that you are slowing down.

Another approach is a module that will flash your tail light when you hit the brake, and then it will turn solid, and then flash, then solid. This is an attention getting device. You be the judge.

And a third approach combines both of the above and works on LED's. Additionally, the flashing time duration, sequence is user adjustable.

LED replacement

This one I like. The newer motorcycles have stock LED tail and brake lights and it is a marked improvement. (You see the same thing on cars.). They are not cheap but I believe it is a wise investment in your personal safety.

You can get a direct, one for one swap out for your taillight. It depends upon your bike model, some just replace the bulb, some replace the bulb and lens. Due to LED technology, heated wiring is not an issue (usually). Overall, this mod is a must for me on any new motorcycle I might buy that does not already have LED's. It really makes a big difference.

Turn Signals

LED Replacement

LED one on one replacement is available and the increase in visibility is significant. Installation is simple, just plug and play (computer talk).

Turn Signal Become Brake Lights too

Just so you are aware of it, there are some modules available that will convert your stock taillights into double duty tail lights and brake lights.

Also, these similar modifications can turn your turn lights into running lights. Google this topic and you will be surprised at all of the variations which are available.

Fun & Games Lights

And finally, so I don't leave anything on the table, here are some fun and games motorcycle lighting goodies;

- License Plate Frame Display Reader: You can program you own special sayings that will display like a ticker tape across the top of the license frame.
- Neon Engine: Purple and blue highlights that accent the engine and whatever else you want to show off at night.
- Valve Stem Lights: When the bike is moving, these create the illusion of your wheels becoming colored circles.

- Etched Windshield lights: You have your favorite image etched into your windshield and then these lights are placed below the windshield, highlighting the image at night.

(Check your motor vehicle laws before going wild with these lighting schemes.)

Bottom Line

Motorcycle lighting is crucial and not only when riding at night. There are some relatively inexpensive lighting upgrades that have significant positive safety impact. Headlight lamp upgrades can improve your range of vision at night without having an adverse impact on the oncoming traffic. LED taillight upgrades will dramatically improve your visibility to those drivers behind you in the daylight. To get the most "Bounce for the Ounce" out of your safety budget, lighting is a great place to spend those dollars.

What Does It Cost?

Headlight Modulator	$70
Headlight lamp upgrade	$15
Headlight light bar add-on	$150 - $250
Tail Light & Brake Light Modulator	$50
LED upgrade, taillight	$100
LED upgrade, turn signals	$25

Resources

Signal Dynamics Corporation	Specializing in lighting products	signaldynamics.com
Custom Dynamics	V-Twin, Chopper, Sport bike or Metric Cruiser	customdynamics.com

Luggage

You want to stop on the way home from work, on your motorcycle, and buy a sandwich to take home. You can forget the soft drink and maybe the French fries. It all depends on how much room you have under the front of your jacket to stuff your dinner inside of your jacket. Go ahead and get the soft drink and try to wedge it between your crotch and gas tank. Let me know how that works out.

Or maybe you are the rider, slowly going down the street with four plastic grocery bags hanging off your rear turn signals or handlebars.

Let's face it, sometimes you are just going to need some luggage to carry stuff with you on your bike.

Luggage includes tool bags, saddlebags, roll bags, rack bags, tank bags, tail bags and T-bags (no, not tea bags). On a sport bike, saddlebags are panniers (pronounced pan-EAR-s). They are made out of fabric, leather, nylon, metal, Fiberglas and sometimes, old milk crates.

They can be permanently attached with bolts, or semi-permanently attached with leather belts and buckles, or nylon straps with quick release clips, or completely detachable with a dozen different quick release techniques.

They can be big, medium or small, black or white or any color you want. They can be rain proof, leak proof, water resistant, lockable, Velcro or buckled, fringed or plain, embossed or natural and finally, cheap or expensive.

Whew! So you get the idea, just about anything you want can be found when it comes to luggage.

Selection Process

The right way to select luggage for your bike is to start by deciding what you want to do on your bike that requires luggage. (TIP: At least put a couple of bungi cords on your bike somewhere until you do get some luggage.)

- Carry tools
- Carry your lunch to work
- Lock up your helmet, carry a spare helmet
- Go on a picnic
- Go for a weekend
- Leave your bike unattended with gear on it
- Carry three bales of hay out to the pasture

All of the above? That's OK, except for the bales of hay; this is my list of luggage needs. The nice thing is that you do not need to put all of this stuff on your bike all of the time (unless you want to, of course). You can put on a few everyday needs and then suit up for that occasional weekender or day ride with your sweetie.

Maybe your list ends after tools. Cool, put all of your tools in a paper grocery bag and roll it up as compact as you can get it and then you will know what size tool bag to buy. Or go the other way around like I did. Choose the tool bag based upon where you want to put it on your motorcycle so it looks cool and then choose only the tools that will fit into the bag.

I like the second way, making the look more important than the practicality. You may favor practicality over the look. That is one thing that is so very individual and so much fun about a motorcycle, you make it the way you want it to please you. It just happens to please me to have other people think my bike looks cool.

Whatever is your priority, get a complete idea of everything you want to eventually get so you can stick with compatible gear (luggage) which will make it easier to maintain and easier to fit on and off as the ride demands. Some vendors offer a complete line from tool bags to cross country serious travel bags. I would not mix up leather with nylon as you do want an overall, somewhat coordinated, look to it all.

For example, here's what I have on my HD Wide Glide.

Tool Bag: On the front forks, above the headlight and touching the bottom of my WindVest wind screen. Instead of using the leather straps that came with it, I am using four (4) large clear plastic tie-wraps to secure the tool bag.

Figure 28 Tool Bag

The bag fits right, looks good, holds my tools and is always attached to my bike. Unlike the sandwich, I don't go anywhere without my tool kit.

I bought an EK-1HD tool kit from Beza Tools for $69.00. Is comes in a roll bag that is designed to fit fork bags. Here's what's in it.

Table 4. Tool Kit List of Tools

Locking pliers	Phillips #1
Tire pressure gauge	Phillips #2
Flashlight w/ Battery	Small Slotted
3/8" Ratchet Driver	Large Slotted
5/8" Spark plug socket	Spark plug gap gauge
13/16" Spark plug socket	Electrical wire

3/8" 7/16" Open-ended wrench	Electrical tape
1/2" 9/16" Open ended wrench	Spare turn / tail light bulb
10mmCombination wrench	Multi-tool
9HexKeys/Allen Wrenches	Mechanic's wire
7-piece Torx set (T-10 -40)	Siphon hose
Shop Towel	Nylon Cable ties (5)

Here is a pretty cool list of stuff you may consider carrying on your bike;

a) Leatherman Tool, 8" Crescent wrench, A stick of anti-seize,

b) A small tube lubricating oil, A tiny bottle of blue Loctite

c) Fuses and Tester, 1157 bulb, Headlight Bulb, Taillight Bulb,

d) Brake Pads, Spark Plugs, Sharp Knife, Electrical Tape, WD-40

e) Can Of Fix A Flat (will work in a tube in a pinch)

f) Sparkplug Gap Gauge, Air Pressure Gauge, CO_2 Tire Inflator,

g) Extra CO_2 Cartridges, Stainless Steel Clamps, Electrical Crimp Ends

h) Air Valve Tool & extra cores, Wire, O_2 Tubing, Hack saw blade

i) Hoses, String, Rubber Gloves, Rag- Towel, Flare,

j) Long Lock cable for coat, bike, etc., Kryptonite Disk Lock,

k) Tissues, Flashlight, Jumper Cables, Kickstand Plate

l) Helmet Cable Lock, Brush, Shield Spray, Visor Cleaner

m) Rain Gear, Wheel Chock, JB Weld 2-Part Epoxy,

n) Superglue, Silicone Grease, Dielectric Grease,
o) Loctite Pipe Sealant-(Seals bleeder threads)
p) Assorted Bolts & Star washers, Pen
q) Cell Phone & Credit Card

Rack Bag: (sold as a Handlebar Bag or what I call my sausage bag) is designed by Saddlemen to be placed on the handlebars like a rolled up sleeping bag. It measures 10" diameter x 14" L, heavy nylon fiber, carrying handle, built-in weatherproof rain cover and shoulder carrying

Figure 29 Sausage Bag

strap. It has all possible combinations of nylon straps with quickie release snaps that I use to secure it to the back of my short sissy bar and it rests on my mini rack. Three snaps and I am off and riding. I use it everyday for my work stuff and running errands. I love this bag.

Saddlebags: Quick release from US Saddlebag Company, are heavy leather, medium size and detach/attach in about three (3) minutes. A small tubular frame attaches to the rear fender struts (permanently) and the saddlebags attach to this frame. When the bags are off, the remaining frame is unobtrusive (doesn't look too bad) and the bike regains it's no saddlebag look, which, of course, is important to me. I usually do not use these bags unless we (my sweetie and I) are going for a day trip or garage sale hopping.

That's it for me. When we go on an overnighter, we load up a large nylon sports bag with our stuff and bungi it to the rack. We have to travel light but hey, so what. I have T-Bags on my wish list but I never seem to get around to getting them. If we were going for a few days, I would spring for T-Bags. I am not really sure why, maybe just because they look cool. I am not sure how they would fit on my short sissy bar.

But what about you, what should you be looking for when it comes to selecting luggage? Let's take a detailed look at all of the various types available.

Tool Bags

There are two basic styles of tool bags. One style is not really a bag until you roll it up. Opened, it is a flat piece of leather and you place your tools on it like knives and forks on a napkin. With everything in place, you fold half of the flat leather over the tools and then roll it up and voilà, a tool bag. The other style is probably what you are already thinking about, a conventional bag. Your tools go inside and then buckle (snap or Velcro) it closed and attach it to your bike.

Tips

- If you are going in and out of your tool bag every day (air pressure gauge) the Velcro closure system is probably what you want.
- Wrap you loose tools in an engine rag (any old dishtowel will do) to keep them from rattling around while you are riding.
- Find a plastic jar that fits inside of your tool bag and then place your tools inside of the plastic jar to keep them moisture free.

- Before you finalize where you are going to secure the tool bag to your bike, test out opening and closing it to make sure it can be easily done, then go ahead and attach it.
- Remember, if it is easy for you to open, it will be easy for anyone else to open it also.

Rack and/or Handlebar Bags

Now we are talking. This bag (to me anyway) may be the greatest piece of motorcycle luggage since sliced bread. Both have all of the pockets and goodies that you can imagine (or you can get them plain if you like). This is a small to medium size bag (you choose the size that matches your bike placement location). It is great to everyday carrying your stuff to work, easy trip to the grocery store, garage sale stuff and so on.

The Rack bag typically will have one or two serious straps on it designed to go around your sissy bar. Additionally, there will be additional tie-down straps to secure the bag to your rack. No rack, no sweat, let it sit on your fender but don't come complaining about your fender getting scratched up.

The handlebar bag gives you the "Then Came Bronson" look of having a sleeping bag rolled up on your handlebars. These do not have the sissy bar straps but usually have all of the straps you need as these bags are designed to fit every combination of forks, handlebars and windshields. Don't be bashful when you see one in your local motorcycle shop. Tell them that you want to take it outside and "fit' it on your bike. Try it out and see how it attaches and how it looks.

Tips
- Weatherproofing is a good idea especially with the handlebar bag. This bag will be receiving the brunt of

the rain and sloppy weather and you will find out that rain will find the smallest pin hole and fill your bag with water.

- If you are considering T-Bags for overnighter trips, check these out before you get a rack bag. Most T-Bags are a kit of two or three bags which include a rack bag. You can avoid buying two rack bags by planning ahead.

Barrel Bags

There are a couple of manufacturers out there who make a rigid style, round bag. It is made in various sizes. This bag is circular shaped like a huge beer can which is placed on its side across your passenger seat. There is a single tie down strap (steel cord) on each end that fixes it to your bike. This bag is usually for solo riding although you can place on your rack and still ride 2-up. The deal with this rigid bag is that it does double duty acting as a backrest when it is in place on your passenger seat. That is a consideration when you are clocking in a few hours on the road. Lumbar (back) support will make a difference on a long trip. The downside is that depending on your bikes height, it may be difficult to swing a leg up and over this bag to get on and off your bike.

The rigid construction will keep stuff inside of the bag from getting crushed like a soft sided bag. So you can put your favorite cowboy hat (or helmet) inside.

Saddlebags

You can make a career out of trying to pick out a pair of saddlebags. In terms of capacity you have three choices, small, medium and large. Small will just about hold your lunch, medium will hold lunch for two and large will handle both lunches and a six-pack of soda. That's it, you can quit thinking in terms of a car trunk, you are on a motorcycle now and if you want to carry a change of clothes, wear two shirts and two pair of Levis. Seriously, you can stuff an amazing amount of goodies into a pair of saddlebags but only if you pack it like a backpack. Backpackers and hikers have already invented this wheel so spend some time in your local sporting goods store and see all of the space saving stuff that is available. No, you will never pack like you are staying in a hotel, but two large saddlebags will hold about the same amount of stuff as an airplane roll-aboard bag.

Narrow Down the Choices

The first thing you want to do to narrow down the choices is to decide it you want a permanently attached or detachable saddlebag. That said, no matter what saddlebags you choose, there are detachable kits that will fit just about any saddlebag. Why detachable? Take them off to keep the clean look of your bike when you don't need saddlebags or take them off to take them with you so no one can steal them or what's inside. So, if you know that you always want your saddlebags on your bike, you have already narrowed down the choices. If you want to quickly remove you saddlebags, keep that in mind when you are looking at bags. You really need to select saddlebags that are made to be detached or will work with one or the detachable systems available.

Your cheapest and easiest choice is to buy some Made-in-China throw-over saddlebags. Leather, maybe, look like saddlebags, yes, any good, what are you kidding me. Unless you really want the Clint Eastwood, "Good, Bad and the Ugly" look with your saddlebags thrown over your shoulder, I suggest avoiding these bags. However, for a cheap throw on solution if you occasionally need some bags, these may be just what the doctor ordered. At least when they get stolen, you will not be out a lot of money.

Placement Considerations

Some saddlebags are made specifically for your bike. They are for the exact model and ensure a great fit. Other saddlebags are generic and will fit numerous bikes and will also not fit numerous bikes.

For example, a HD Dyna model has the rear shocks/springs on the outside of the rear wheel, right where the saddlebags go. These saddlebags have the inside of the bag molded around the shock so the bag will mount flat against the bike, covering most of the shock. The HD Softtail has the rear shock mounted under the swing arm/frame and there are no external outside shocks where the saddlebags go. These Softtail saddlebags have more interior room as they do not need to allow for the shock placement. The Dyna style bags are not a good fit on the Softtail and visa versa.

Generic saddlebags are built for both configurations, outside springs or no outside springs. Be careful and make sure to get the bags that fit your bike.

Another size consideration is the exhaust on your bike. You may have stock exhaust pipes of something a little more exotic. Make sure that your new saddlebags have enough exhaust pipe clearance to keep the exhaust pipes from burning up your bags.

And finally, watch out for clearance on your turn signals. Back to the Harley example, if you want large bags which will be placed right over the existing turn signals, you will need to make a modification. You can either relocate the turn signals 2 to 4 inches towards the rear of the fender (they sell kits for this) or you may decide to remove the turn signals from the fender mounts altogether and place a turn signal "bar" across the license plate area. Again, they sell kits for this also. Don't forget about the wiring issues, relocating turn signals 2 to 4 inches has minimal wiring, placing a license plate bar is more involved. Both choices are pretty easy for a non-professional (like myself) and can be easily accomplished without buying any special tools or whatnot. The relocation kit generally will have everything you need in terms of parts.

The decision comes down to cosmetic and bag size. How bad do you want those large bags and what do you want your bike to look like after you are finished. For example, my HD Wide Glide (Dyna series with outside springs) is a street bike and I love the street bike look. I want quick release saddlebags for those weekend rides with my sweetie but during the week, I do not want any bags (read un-cool, non-street look) hanging off my bike. So when I chose my bags, I did not want to get stuck relocating my turn signals to a license plate bar. The license plate bar belongs to the "Bagger" look, not the "Street" bike look. Picky, you bet cha.

Figure 30 Saddlebag

To Lock or Not To Lock

When I started riding, I wanted to lock up everything. Paranoid, well maybe, but I just did not want anyone to steal anything if I could help it. Since then, I have changed my attitude.

One morning I found my bike cover sliced open and my saddlebags wide open with everything inside gone. My good chaps, my cable lock, my winter gloves and even my empty glasses case were gone.

The bags did not have locks and I wonder if that would have made the difference. Who knows, but I did learn not to leave anything in my bags overnight. In fact, I learned that my new quick detachable bags were coming off the motorcycle at night and enjoying the comfort of the inside of my house. Problem solved, I take the bags inside at night.

I can do the same when staying overnight in a motel, eliminating any chance of anyone stealing anything out of my bags. More likely, I will get a first floor room and roll my motorcycle inside the room for the night (just don't tell the desk clerk that this is your plan).

Locks (to me at least) will only keep the honest people out of your bags. The dedicated thief will probably overcome the locks and then not only will your stuff be gone but your bags will be screwed up where the locks were jimmied.

But that's only my opinion; you may have real value to getting locks on your saddlebags. If so, try to get combination locks so you can avoid the extra key issue.

Solid or hard shell saddlebags are a natural for locks and almost always come with locks installed.

Let's Go Saddlebag Shopping

Now that you have considered the bike specific placement issues shocks, turn signals and exhaust pipes, you have narrowed down the field. Next you must take a look at what material you want textile, leather or hard shell.

Textile:

Tough, durable, weather resistant and cheaper than leather but does it have the look? Check them out, and I mean go to your local motorcycle shop and put your hands on these. Take them outside and hold them against your bike and see what they look like on your bike.

Leather:

Traditional and all of the qualities of textile but with fewer bells and whistles than textile bags may have. More expensive than textile and they will require maintenance to keep them supple and weather resistant for years to come. Again, put your hands on them and try them out on your bike before you decide.

Hard Shell:

There are usually designed to fit an exact model of bike. They have a unique look and are very durable and weather proof. Not weather resistant like leather and textile, but weather proof. Now leather and textile can become weatherproof but not without some additional stuff involved. The best way to check out these hard shell bags is to find someone who has them on their bike, parked outside of the supermarket, the swap meet and so on. Don't be bashful, go up to the rider and ask "How do you like these bags?" Usually, the owner is proud of the bags and will give you the scoop.

By shopping at your local MC shops, motorcycle meets and shows and on the internet, you will narrow down your choices and know what you want. Once you have decided on a bag that will fit your bike, it's all about price.

Shop the internet and print out a page with your desired bag with specs and the price. Take this down to your local

MC shop and start haggling with the salesperson. If you can order it over the internet, usually your local MC shop can order it as well. If the MC shop will sell it to you for the same (or lower) price, you have found it. Don't forget about internet shipping and taxes (or lack of taxes). Also be aware of the internet company's return policy. With all of that in mind, you will know what the best deal is.

More Saddlebag Issues

Some brands of saddlebags have belt buckle closures with longer than necessary belts. This extra length is intended to allow you to place your leather jacket (too big to stuff inside) on top of the bag and secure it by running these belts over the jacket. This is great when the day gets too hot and you (and your sweetie) want to take off your jackets.

Conchos, studs and fringe are your way of making your bags your individual statements. Whatever your taste may be, you can get bags with these decorative items or put them on yourself later.

You can put just about any saddlebag on your bike, somehow, someway but remember when you sell that bike; it may not be worth your while to keep those bags for your new bike. When buying a used bike, always try to get the saddlebags thrown in on the deal. It may not increase the price of the used bike by very much but it may save you $500 by not needing to purchase new bags.

More Bags

The tank bag is normally a spots bike accessory but you may find that a tank bag is just what you are looking for. These tank bags attach to your gas tank using magnets. The bag surface between the magnets and the tank is mad of soft, grip able material that will not scratch your tanks paint (at least that's the theory). These tank bags come in various sizes and with various features including a plastic window on the top for your map. I like the map idea. If you think one of these bags will do the job for you, you must take it out of the shop and try it on your tank first to ensure a proper fit.

Another bag is the windshield bag which is a small bag and handy for your glasses and stuff, keeping everything within easy reach.

There are other shapes and styles of bags available. Remain creative about this stuff. Just because a bag was made to be a sissy bar bag doesn't mean that will not work as a fork tool bag.

What Does It Cost?

Tool Bag	$50
Rack/Handlebar Bag	$75
Saddlebags	$150 - $650

Resources

Leather Works, Inc.	Leading manufacturer of motorcycle bags. Home of the Buffalo Head nickel bags.	leatherworksinc.com
Saddlemen	Leading manufacturer of motorcycle seats and bags.	saddlemen.com
Beza Tools	Tool Kits: We create cutting edge, solution-oriented products for people from all walks of life.	beza.biz
US Saddlebag Co.	At U.S. Saddlebag Co. we go to great lengths to create superior products, using only the highest standards and finest materials to construct our leather goods.	ussaddlebag.com

Seat

What's the big deal on a seat? A seat is a seat, sit down and go. This is what I thought and it is what a lot of riders think. I have found out that the seat can really make a significant difference in your riding enjoyment and in this chapter I am going to tell you all about your options.

The two biggest considerations are seat height and seat comfort. These are not separate issues but combined and can make or break your ride. A low seat that gets your feet flat on the ground at a stop light may be very uncomfortable after 100 miles on the highway. Conversely, a comfortable long distance highway seat may leave you on your tiptoes at that same stop light.

What's Good For You?

What's good for me may not be good for you and visa versa. You may be a very happy camper with the stock setup on your bike and not even be interested in reading about all of this seat stuff. If so, well that's great. Go get on your motorcycle and have fun.

Seats play an important role in enjoying your ride. To me, it's part of the big three: Handlebars, mid or forward foot controls and the seat. They all work together to get you into the right riding posture to make you comfortable and minimize fatigue on long rides.

It's worth it to read on and make sure that you have not overlooked anything. Make sure that you are not missing out on some simple steps that may make a big difference in your ride.

Body Size

Well we all come in different sizes and shapes. Some of us are tall with short legs, short with long legs and so on. Riders with long legs are usually OK with stock seats as far as being flat footed at the stop light. Riders with short legs usually learn to "make-do" with what they have and just go for it. I am average height (5' 9") with a 32" inseam on my Levis. I like to be low on the bike and I have 10" risers and forward foot controls. I like to ride upright, even a little lean back, arms pretty straight out in front of me and my feet towards the front of the bike. This is pretty typical for cruisers.

> I had a Suzuki Intruder 1400 (Harley looking cruiser) and I fit pretty well into the stock handlebars, upgraded Mustang seat and forward controls. I put about 20,000 miles on it just like that and rarely even thought about changing anything. I was satisfied.

I took the time with my later bike to get everything right and I have to tell you it really made a difference. Those 20,000 just OK miles on the Suzuki Intruder would have been twenty thousand very much more enjoyable miles.

There is a winning combination for you too. It may even be the stock combination but until you swing a leg up and over the seat, you will never know. Yep, you have to try sitting on a number of different seats to figure out what seat is the best for you.

Riding Style

I am writing this directly towards cruisers. I want to just sit down on a motorcycle and go for a ride. I do not want to climb up, suit up, bend over, plug in or whatever else you have to do to go ride a Sport bike (or any other non-cruiser, style motorcycle).

Sometimes I just want to ride down to the local supermarket to get some bread and milk. Sometimes, I am commuting to work and fighting the daily rush hour traffic. And sometimes, I am with my sweetie taking a Saturday ride through the city (we call it the urban tour) or just heading off into the mountains with no destination in mind.

So my riding style calls for an all around seat, with a passenger pillion (2-Up). A seat that is comfortable on a long ride but not a Barcalounger for riding around town.

Seat Height

Seat height is a product of the motorcycle design (frame) and the actual seat itself. For example, I have always been interested in a BMW road bike but for me, the seat height has been the contract breaker. The BMW frame makes for a tall seat and for me personally (I am 5′ 9″), it is just too tall. I like to have my feet flat on the ground when I am sitting at a light.

Feet Flat On The ground

Having my feet flat on the ground not only feels right, but it allows me more control when I am maneuvering the motorcycle around into a tight parking spot. "Walking" the motorcycle is always a challenge and when your feet are not really reaching the ground in the first place, it can result in a motorcycle lying on its side. For me, anything under 5 mph is the most difficult maneuvers and the better foot control, the better maneuverability.

With a BMW for example, no matter how low of a seat you put on the motorcycle, the frame height is going to keep me up on my tiptoes when I am standing at a red light.

However, I see 5′ 6″ motorcycle cops maneuvering the same BMW around like it is a piece of cake. The BMW's smaller tires and center of balance compensates for the tall seat. And, the BMW enthusiasts will tell you that the seat height is exactly where you want if for a true road bike ride.

But this book is not about BMW's, it about cruisers so let's get some Harley specifications here as examples.

Table 5. Seat Height

Motorcycle	Seat Height (Inches)
2006 HD Softtail Deluxe FLSTN/I	24.5
2006 HD Dyna Low Rider FXDLI	25.2
2006 HD Fat Boy FLSTF/I	25.4
2006 HD Heritage Softtail Classic FLSTC/I	25.5
2006 HD Dyna Street Bob FXDBI	25.8
2006 HD Sportster XL1200L	26.25

The Softtail comes with the lowest stock seat height, then, getting taller, is the Dyna and finally, the tallest of them all is the Sportster. All of these can be changed so if your heart is set on a Street Bob (Dyna) but the seat is too tall for your tastes, don't get discouraged, you can make it fit you.

Sitting On Top of the Motorcycle or being Part of the Motorcycle

There is another seat height consideration that is very important to me. When I was on my Sportster with the stock seat, I always felt like I was sitting on top of the motorcycle.

I mean, I felt like I was literally, on top of the motorcycle like a big piece of luggage tied to the seat. Then I replaced the stock seat with a lower profile seat, lowering the seat height about 1 1/2″ and I felt like I was more in tune with the motorcycle. I was more "connected". I was a happy camper and forgot about seats until a couple of years later when I bought a Dyna Wide Glide.

When I bought the Wide Glide, I started out looking at the Street Bob. I felt good on the Street Bob, stock, with no modifications, it was just right. I loved it; however, I could not get the extended front fork with the street Bob which I just had to have. It was only available on the Wide Glide.

I bought the Wide Glide, replaced the stock seat with a Mustang low profile seat and lowered the bike 1" (replaced the stock shocks but that's another story). Now, I had it all. My feet were flat on the ground at the stoplight, I felt like I had control and maneuverability but most of all, I was no longer a piece of baggage strapped to the top of the seat. I was into the motorcycle itself. I felt like I was part of the bike. I had found the right combination of frame height and seat that made me and the motorcycle a team. You need to do the same thing with your bike.

Low Profile Seat

At this point you should have figured out how tall your current seat is and how much you want to lower it. Bolt on seats (exact replacement for the stock seat), will drop the seat height 1 to 1 1/2 inches without getting into the comfort zone. More than 1 1/2 inches and you will be riding on a hard seat and you rear end will never let you forget it. Maybe you just zip around town for thirty minutes at a time and a hard seat is OK but if you are heading out for a hundred mile highway ride, a hard seat will be very uncomfortable.

Modifying Your Stock Seat

I did that. I modified the seat on my nifty, thrifty Honda Fifty about forty years ago. I found a block of foam rubber, a chunk of Naughide and viola, my new modified seat. Just sitting on it would depress the foam so much you could feel the bolts in your rear end. Hitting a bump in the road at speed was brutal. I ride that seat to school for a year. I am older and wiser (maybe more delicate) now.

When researching this book, I have seen web sites illustrating how to cut down your stock seat. Basically, you remove the cover, use a heat knife to cut down the foam, and then replace the cover. It looks to me like the critical thing is accurate measurements on the foam to be cut down. If you do it right, for a very low investment, you can turn your existing stock seat into a low profile seat. Will it be comfortable? Who knows but if you are committed to getting a low profile seat on your motorcycle, why not try to modify the stock seat and see what happens. If it is screwed up, you were going to buy a replacement seat anyway. If it comes out good, you just saved $300 or $400 bucks.

Narrow Seats

Getting your seat lower is one thing but do not forget about the width of the seat. Specifically, the front half of the seat that is against the insides of your legs when you are stopped and standing up over the seat is the critical area. If this part of the seat is too wide, your legs are spread apart and can't reach as far down towards the ground as you want them to reach. By narrowing this part of the seat, you legs can come together and extend their downward length to the ground. If you do this right, you will leave the rear part of the seat which holds your rear end alone so while you are riding you never even notice the narrower part of the seat.

This is a very effective way of getting your feet flat on the ground even when the seat is not as low as you would like it to be.

Harley Seats

Start at the beginning. If you have a Harley, check out what the Harley dealer has to offer. If there is a HD seat that looks good to you, check your local HD shops for your model which has that seat on it. Sit down and see what it's all about. Some dealers will put the new seat on a floor model so you can test it out in the showroom. After all, it's very easy to remove a late model HD seat and pull one off the wall and put it on.

Figure 31 Stock Seat

Currently HD has a pretty good selection of genuine HD seats. Lots of goodies tailored for all kinds of riders. If you live in an area with more than one HD shop, take the Saturday tour and check them all out. Talk to the dealers and ask them how they like this or that seat. Do they ride on it? What seat do they use and so on? If you ask enough, you will start to hear trends pointing towards one seat and away from another.

Once you have found the seat of your dreams, take a look online and see what's out there. Riders are changing seats all of the time and at any given moment, the seat of your dreams has just been replaced by the seat of someone else's dreams and is now sitting in their garage. You may be pleasantly surprised to get a relatively new HD seat for 1/3 of the dealer's price. Like my dad used to tell me, "Shop around son".

I hear people saying that the stock Harley seats just are no good. Uncomfortable, they don't weather very well and so on. The theory is that HD puts a low quality seat on hoping that you will spend the cash to upgrade to a more profitable seat (profitable to HD that is). I also hear folks saying they have put 50K miles on the stock HD seat with no problem. Personally, I only have had my rear end in a HD seat for a lot of miles with no problem so I just don't know. You make the call.

Used Seats

You may find a used seat that suits your needs. It is important to get a replacement seat for your stock seat that has been made to fit your exact model of motorcycle. So unless you get lucky, eBay and Craig's list are not going to be a very good source. Close is not good enough. Sure, I can take a seat and bolt it on just like you can but I will not be swapping it out very easily later on. When I want to do something with the electronics or wiring harness (usually under the seat) I am again going to spend some time on the seat. If you do find a used seat, make sure it is the correct fit. And don't forget the "cool" factor, a Suzuki seat bolted on your Fat Boy will turn some heads, and get a few chuckles too.

Make sure to check the model year as things change from year to year. My 2006 Wide Glide has a different seat pan width that earlier Wide Glides. HD changed the width of the rear fender in 2006 and the seat pan width changed with the fender.

> *NOTE: HD seats have a single screw on the rear of the seat (thumb screw available) and a seat tongue under the front of the seat which makes seat removal a 3 minute job. Sissy bars and luggage racks can complicate it, if they are in the way. This is a great feature, and I do not want to lose it by bolting a non-standard seat with non-standard bolts and clamps.*

You can save a bunch of cash by buying a used seat if you are willing to do the legwork and if you can find one that fits your bike.

Tips

- Is it real leather? Here's a simple test. Use your a right hand finger to press down on the web part of your left hand between your thumb and first finger. As you press, you will see your skin wrinkle up in a star burst shape outward from the pressing finger. OK, leather is skin also, so to test leather, press your finger into it and look for the same wrinkle pattern to emerge. If it wrinkles appear, its leather, if they do not appear, its Naughide.

Manufacturers

There are about a zillion choices out there and figuring out what is best for you can be an expensive trial and error adventure. I am going to narrow down the choices for you. Between these three manufacturers you can find just about every possible seat style and configuration out there. As with most motorcycle parts, it is too expensive for dealers to stock more than a few samples so you have to do your legwork to get your hands on one. Motorcycle shows are a great place to see (and touch) all of the stuff that you cannot find in your local stores.

I have found that there are three major manufacturers of seats that always seem to get high reviews from riders I know: Mustang, Corbin and Saddlemen. Here's what I like about these three.

CORBIN

I have never owned a Corbin but I have seen plenty of them and I am impressed. Corbin does use leather and has some trick stuff in addition to the complete line of seats. They have a flip up "convertible" sissy bar type of passenger seat that is worth a look. They also have a heater option which is very interesting.

MUSTANG

I have had three Mustang replacement seats on three different motorcycles and I am 100% happy will all three. They do not sell any leather seats but a composite vinyl that looks like leather. And it really does look like leather. My motorcycles have always been outside 24/7 and I have never had any fade or weather problems with these seats. They are high quality and they look like they were made for the motorcycle. I mean really made for the motorcycle. Normal or low profile, they hold their shape and are very comfortable. On a long ride, I do not ever find myself thinking about the seat. I really like Mustang seats.

SADDLEMEN

I use their tool bags but I have never owner one of their seats. I have heard some good stuff about them from fellow riders. In particular, one friend ordered a custom seat with narrow sides and when he got the seat, he did not like it.

Saddlemen took it back and reworked it until he was happy. He now swears by Saddlemen.

Lower the Motorcycle

If you have a Sportster and are currently at 26.25 inches with the stock seat, about the best you can do is get it down to 25 inches or maybe 24.5 inches. Still too tall, well the next option is to lower the bike. In my opinion, if you are looking for a Sportster which is below 24.5 inches seat height, you should trade it in on another model which has the ability to go lower. Investing $300 or $400 in a seat and finding out that it is still too tall will be a big disappointment. Lowering a Sportster is not an easy effort for a newbie.

In fact lowering any motorcycle is a complex undertaking and unless you know what you are doing you have a good chance of screwing up the handling ability of the motorcycle. Usually, you will replace the rear shocks with shorter shocks, shorten the front fork by replacing the fork springs and then modifying your kickstand so your bike will stand up on it's own after all of the lowering modifications. It's not cheap. To have an experienced motorcycle mechanic do the work, parts and labor can run close to $1000 or more before you are done.

Tips

- Find a local motorcycle dealer (doesn't have to be HD) and ask them about lowering your bike. Make sure they have experience in this area and you may be pleasantly surprised.

And again, once you start screwing around with the bikes length and ground clearance, you are running a risk of taking away the bikes handling ability. This could be more than just annoying, it could be dangerous.

Seat Comfort

Soft is not necessarily comfortable. It's a great looking seat and it feels very soft and comfortable sitting there in the shop. 200 miles later, your rear end is talking to you and it's not saying what you want to hear. "Come on Frank, give me a break! This seat is killing me!"

I used to wonder how in the world these championship bicycle riders could put in ten or twelve hours on that skinny little hard bicycle seat. Now I know the seat is built to match the body, not the perception of the rider. I discovered this after putting in my first two hundred mile day on my new Mustang replacement seat.

Out of the box, the Mustang seat looked very cool. Heavy duty leather (actually vinyl), tight seams, fits perfectly and it really set the look of the bike. However, it felt hard to the touch. I could depress the seat with my fingers but it was not the soft, inviting, pillow I had envisioned.

It fit well when I sat down. It felt secure and comfortable. It wasn't hard like metal but it was really stiff. The stock seat had a diamond tuff design (Suzuki Intruder 1400) and was way soft compared to this Mustang seat. Oh well, I looked cool and I have already paid for it so I might as well give it a chance.

> 200 miles later I was almost back home after taking a ride up to Reno and back when I realized that I had not thought about my new seat since I left Reno, 100 miles ago.

That was when I understood the hard bicycle seat. I had not thought about my new seat because it was doing its job and doing it so well that it was transparent to the ride.

Short Ride or Long Ride?

To me this is like proving a negative. If the seat is good for a long ride, it probably is good for a short ride. The negative part is if it is good for a short ride, who knows if it is any good for a long ride.

Now I am eliminating all of the custom choppers, Big Dogs, hard tails and the like because those are very special bikes that are rarely on a long distance ride. I am talking about the average Harley rider who may do 400 miles in one day a couple of time a year. OK, maybe 20 times a year. OK, maybe every weekend. You get the picture.

I want an all around seat that is comfortable going to the corner store or roundtrip to San Francisco (I live in Sacramento). I want it to look cool. That's right; I want it to look cool. No dork seats allowed. I also want it to hold up under the weather, especially the neighborhood car wash. No fading, no tearing, and did I say, it must look cool. I want the functionality of a combat motorcycle seat, imagine Hummer made the seat, but the sleek, cool look of a custom alligator low profile, street seat.

And there's the rub. The cooler it looks, the more uncomfortable it is. You just cannot have it both ways, there's always a compromise.

Riding 2-Up

Figure 32 Seat Components

Now I am going to make things more complicated by adding in the requirement that I want to take my sweetie with me now and then. So here comes the pillion.

*Pillion: A pad or cushion for an extra rider behind
the saddle on a horse or motorcycle.*

Not only do I want a pillion, but I want one that is
comfortable. I have a saying in my family, "When momma is
happy, everybody is happy" and that really holds true when
riding on the back of the motorcycle.

> We were both in the local Harley shop checking out
> this very cool 2004 Wide Glide, lowered, built out,
> nice paint, lots of chrome and a beautiful Corbin seat.
> It was a low profile seat, tan leather (matching the
> paint) with a "courtesy" pillion or passenger seat. The
> pillion was about 4 or 5 inches wide and tapered
> down in the rear matching the contour of the fender
> and looked almost invisible, keeping the cool look of
> the bike. I sat on it and asked her to get on and try it
> out. She did, briefly, and then she got off. I didn't
> even ask, the look on her face said it all. Scratch that
> idea Frank and move on to the real passenger seat.
> That doesn't mean its not a great seat for you, it just
> will not work for the two of us.

There additional passenger considerations when selecting
your seat. The passenger does not have the feet flat on the
ground issue so the height of the passenger pillion is open.
Think about the passengers' height (if you plan on having
the same passenger most of the time). You are going to be
sitting lower than the passenger. The passenger (again,
depending on height) will be looking into the back of your
helmet or over the top of your helmet. Looking into the back
of your helmet is pretty boring but it does block a lot of
wind. Looking over your helmet has a better view but gets
the same wind blast as the driver (you). Get a tall pillion to

allow the passenger to look over the helmet if that is your goal.

The next thing is the pillion width. You can get a touring seat with 10 inches or more of width which will make your passenger happy but will look pretty goofy when you are riding alone. I think 8 inches is adequate and depending on your motorcycle rear fender width, 8 inches doesn't look too bad.

It is time to start thinking about a sissy bar. Your passenger will appreciate having something there to stop from sliding backwards during acceleration. There are all kinds of sissy bars and some of them will conflict with some seats. The conflict is usually a large pillion pad pressed into the base of the sissy bar which looks sloppy and also makes removing the seat an additional hassle.

As with all of this seat information, there is no substitute for trying it out. Having said that, how do you try out a seat that is just a picture on some web page? Here's how;

- Visit your local motorcycle shops, American and metric, and see if they have what you are looking for.
- Attend the local motorcycle shows and see if the seat vendors have it. Don't forget to walk around the motorcycle parking area and check out what everyone else is using for a seat. This is a goldmine of ideas.
- Check out the online forums, searching for exactly that seat. Most likely someone else has experience with the seat and has posted some comments. If not, ask. You will be surprised how helpful fellow riders are in these forums.

Buy it online after reading and understanding the vendors return policy. Worst case you may be out $15 or $20 for shipping.

Switching Seats

I seriously considered switching seats as a solution and a lot of folks do switch out seats as often as the mood strikes them. The concept is to get a great solo seat for your commute or solo riding and then have a complete touring seat for riding 2-up. Not bad. The Harley seat can be replaced with a finger tightened screw and you are ready to go in a few minutes.

It gets a little more complicated when you add a luggage rack and/or a sissy bar. But that still only means that it is a little cramped getting your hand on the screw, maybe add a few more minutes.

For me, I don't trust the hand tightened screw; I want to get a wrench on it. This makes it even a little more complicated and adds a couple more minutes. But this approach is still reasonable if you want to change seats for a weekend or infrequent 2-up ride.

Maybe I am just lazy but it all seems like a hassle and I elected to get a seat that would be a compromise between comfort and coolness. Finding such a seat was not as easy as it sounds.

It is appropriate to mention that there is a product out there that is a temporary, suction cup pillion seat. Just stick it on and away you go. I do not have any first hand experience with these but I am sure that they fill a niche for some folks just fine. Maybe you are single, and the opportunity arises to give someone from the opposite sex a ride. There you go, just stick it on and, wait a minute, hold on, you have to have the suction cup pillion with you if you want to use it, maybe in a tool bag or gear bag strapped to your handlebars? And of course, in most states, you will need a helmet for your rider so maybe it is in the gear bag (forget the tool bag, too small) or also strapped onto your handlebars.

Sounds like too much hassle for me. I don't even want to have an extra helmet sticking on the bike somewhere, no matter how unobtrusive it appears. I'll pass.

Seat Styles

I am looking for a low profile solo seat and a comfortable passenger pillion and here's what's available out there. There are examples of the basics. You will find numerous variations from numerous manufacturers. Plus, you can (for a price) have just about anything you want built to your specifications. Remember, your HD is your canvas and you are the artist.

What Seat Do I Have?

I ended up with the Mustang Custom Squareback™. A low cut seat for the driver and a squared-off passenger seat. Here is my thought process for arriving at this decision for all of you who have not yet read enough about seats.

I started looking for a seat as soon as I bought my 2006 Wide Glide. My previous experience taught me that finding a low profile seat that still afforded my wife some degree of pillion comfort was a difficult task.

I went to a local shop (Seat Works, Sacramento, CA) and made a deal with the owner. He was going to use the stock seat plate and build a new foam body on it making it low profile and increasing the pillion area. To make a long story short, I got hosed on the deal ($560) and ended up with a seat that looked cool and started falling apart after three weeks riding. I returned to the shop only to find new occupants who had no clue how to reach the previous tenant. Oh well, live and learn.

Now I had a new motorcycle with a ratty seat and I searched the Internet for my dream seat. My seat problem was further compounded by the fact that in 2006, HD made the Wide Glide rear fender wider than previous years and the existing inventory of seats would not fit. Each manufacturer needed to retool for the new width except Mustang who had seats in stock ready to ship the next day.

I ordered the Squareback as it promised a low profile and relatively large pillion pad. I received it right away, put it on and have not looked back since then. That was

Figure 33 Mustang Squareback Seat

about 15,000 miles ago. It was $300 and I consider that $300 to be well spent.

Bottom Line

If your stock seat works for you, forget about upgrading your seat. If you want to improve your bike's look or your personal comfort, upgrade the seat.

Check with your manufacturer first and then look into after-market seats. Make sure that any seat you buy is designed to fit your exact make and model of bike.

What Does It Cost?

Harley Davidson seats	$300 and up
After market seats	$300 and up

Resources

Corbin	Leading manufacturer of motorcycle seats	corbin.com
Mustang	Leading manufacturer of motorcycle seats	mustangseats.com
Saddlemen	Leading manufacturer of motorcycle seats	saddlemen.com
Harley Davidson Forums	Harley Davidson discussion forum and one stop resource for all Harley Davidson related discussions	hdforums.com
Motorcycle Cruiser Forum	Motorcycle Enthusiast to discuss your motorcycle, places to ride motorcycles, latest bikes and accessories, shows & events	motorcyclecruiser.com
V-Twin Forum	Welcome to V-Twin Forum the best hang-out for V-Twin owners of Harley Davidson, Buell and Victory motorcycles	v-twinforum.com/forums

There is a whole bunch more manufacturers and they range from very inexpensive to unbelievably expensive with alligator, lizard and snake skin designs, and gel seats, inflatable, back rests and so on.

There are a lot of forums out there. Check them out. You can "lurk" in the background and get a feel for the kind of stuff that is going on there. Posting a question on these forums is like having a 24 hr support hotline. Just remember to take the information offered with a grain of salt.

Security

The way I look at motorcycle security is that there are a lot of folks out there who want my motorcycle. Well, I want my motorcycle too. It comes down to who wants it the most. If I really want to keep it, I better do whatever I can to do keep it. I know a few motorcycle owners who say, "Hey, I've got insurance. If they steal it, they steal it. My insurance will get me a replacement."

I like my motorcycle, I don't want a replacement. If somehow, even with my best efforts, one of those other guys is successful in stealing my motorcycle, well I will be glad that I do have insurance and then, I will want a replacement. But I still like my motorcycle and I am going to take every reasonable step to keep it.

When I first got it with less than 5 miles on it, I treated it like everyone in the world was going to steal it. I had to leave it overnight in our apartment's carport area. Nice apartment complex but still, I had neighbors who had their cars stolen out of the same carport area so I was on red alert. One of the first things I bought was a HD security chain and heavy duty padlock so I could chain it to the carport cover support (pole). I bought a HD motorcycle cover so it would not be so visible. I actually parked it in front of my car in the same parking slot. My theory was that it would be less visible. We lived on the third floor and I could just see one side of the locked up motorcycle from our bathroom window. I laugh now at all of the trips I made to that window to see if it was still there after hearing any noise in the night.

After a few restless nights, I decided that my new HD security chain was not enough. Due to the physical layout of the parking spot and the carport cover pole, the only way I could get the chain around both the carport pole and the motorcycle was by running it through the front wheel. In bed at night I imagined professional motorcycle thieves arriving in a utility truck complete with every quick release tool known to man. They would be on the bike and have it in their truck in less than 10 seconds, without making any sound whatsoever.

I was off to the hardware store where I bought 8 feet of 2 inch chain. I also got 6 feet of rubber tubing to go around the outside of the chain and prevent scratching my motorcycle. I added two heavy duty locks and I was off to chain up my motorcycle.

Now I could move the bike into a better position so I could see more of it from the bathroom window (so what?) and instead of running the chain through the front wheel, I could run it around the frame under the engine. That with the stock fork lock and the stock engine disable switch had it locked up pretty good. I always covered it at night even if I had to come back downstairs after letting the pipes cool for twenty minutes.

Later, I lie in bed thinking about those same professional thieves only now they came equipped with huge bolt cutters, aerosol cans of Freon or nitrogen (freeze the padlock and shatter it with a hammer). The bike cover did not have a HD logo but it was the traditional black top with silver lower heat material. Anyone with any experience would know there was a Harley inside.

Total security, hardly, but there is a happy ending to my story. After six years, I have never lost a motorcycle. I still have the same chain and locks. I have been lucky. I have had cover slashed and my saddle bags emptied.

I believe that the best security probably can be overcome by four big guys and a pair of bolt cutters. The more security steps you take, the longer a thief will need to steal it and the more likely you motorcycle will still be there in the morning.

Tips

- Lock it with a high quality heavy chain and heavy locks.
- Put the chain through the frame, not the wheels.
- Always disable the ignition.
- Always cover your bike with a generic $20 cover that looks like a $20 cover over a $300 motorcycle.
- Add disc locks if you have the self discipline to put them on and take them off every time.
- Don't get too confident with it inside of your garage, at least lock the fork and disable the ignition. I would probably even use a chain inside of the garage.

Yeah, I know, it's a pain in the rear but remember there is probably someone out there who wants your motorcycle. The winner is the one who gets to keep it.

$200 Helmet: Gone in 60 Seconds

After the first two weeks with your new motorcycle and your new helmet, the day will come when you start getting tired of carrying your helmet into the grocery store or flopping it down on the restaurant table, announcing to the world that , "Yeah Buddy, that's my bike outside and I am the real deal!" Relax, nobody is noticing you and your helmet is not turning any heads.

The helmet thrill is gone and now you want to know what you do with your helmet when you leave your bike unattended at the cinema, the grocery store or the swap meet. You first solution is to take your new, expensive, shinny helmet with you when you leave your bike. But after lugging your helmet around with you for a couple of hours, you start looking for a more practical solution.

You have seen bikes parked allover the place with the helmet either sitting on the seat or hanging from the handlebars. OK, problem solved, just leave your helmet on the bike and put your faith in human nature that it will still be there when you return.

We (us riders) all understand that no-one will want to steal a used helmet because savvy riders would never trust their skull to a helmet with unknown history. Maybe it has been dropped and the lining has cracked inside, rendering it dangerous when you need it the most. However, non-savvy riders and all others either do not know about the cracked liner theory or they just do not give a darn. It is shiny, obviously expensive, looks cool and even if there is no street sale value, it would look good hanging on the wall, so it is at risk.

If you just cannot part with your helmet, let's go shopping for a backpack that will hold your helmet, leaving you hands free to enjoy the swap meet.

There are three (3) ways to secure your helmet:
1. carry or backpack it with you
2. install a helmet lock
3. use a security cable

Let's take a look at the backpacks.

Shoei, Firstgear and Icon (Urban & Squad) backpacks, above, are three examples of helmet backpacks. There are a lot more out there and they will run you between $80 and $100.

I was looking at buying a backpack when I first started riding again. Not just for the helmet issue, but to use a backpack instead of saddlebags for my daily work commute.

Gotta put your lunch somewhere, eh? And a couple of times I used my old hiking backpack to carry my helmet while I was walking around at the local swap meet. I didn't like it. Not your cup of tea either? I like riding to the cinema or shopping for the inherent motorcycle freedom, not to be saddled like a donkey, or worst yet, a goofball. OK, OK, just my opinion, whatever floats you boat is good with me.

So, we are back with leaving your helmet on the bike. How about locking it to the bike itself? At least it will keep the honest people from stealing your helmet.

Let look at some helmet locks. First of all, you may already have a helmet lock on you bike. If your bike is Japanese, it may have a lock. I had a Suzuki Intruder 1400 (Harley knock-off) which had two helmet locks, right and left side on the rear fender. Unfortunately, after I put on saddlebags, the locks ended up under the bags and were difficult to use.

Some bikes (like my 2003 Sportster) use a padlock on the front fork neck to lock the bike (the newer Harleys have built in locks) so you are already dealing with an extra lock every time you want to leave your bike somewhere. The hassle is not with locking the bike; it's carrying the lock around with you everywhere you go. The old style bikers usually lock it onto their Levis belt loop but if you are carrying a cell phone and the rest of the urban biker stuff, this is a pain.

However, if you have a padlock and must use it, the easiest way to lock your helmet is to use a lock extension with your padlock. Simply stick the extension through the "D" rings on your helmet and the other end goes on the padlock. You may be able to padlock directly to the "D" rings but usually, there is not enough room to get your helmet in close to the padlock. These extensions solve that problem.

Next choice is add-on helmet locks. There are two basic types, clamp on and screw on. There are a lot of different choices and manufacturers out there. The basic idea with these locks is to attach the lock to your bike and then lock your helmet with the "D" rings in the lock. You need to carry a key with you when you are riding.

The Kuryakyn KewLock attaches to your handlebar ends and is pretty cool. I would get two, one for each end. Not just for cosmetic reasons but to balance the handlebars.

Next comes a simple metal leash or cord that you run through the "D" rings (or chin guard) and then around some part of your bike.

Whatever you do choose, remember, you will need to carry the lock with you when you are riding.

Masterlock has a 2 foot retractable cable and combination lock. Lock your helmet and maybe your jacket. No keys to worry about but you need to carry the lock with you when you are riding.

So what do I use? Which one of these marvelous solutions do I actually use? Well, none actually. I usually leave my helmet hanging on the handlebars and cross my fingers that it will still be there when I return. I do carry a small tool bag combo handlebar bag (12" X 18"), which attaches to the rear of my sissy bar and rests on the small fender rack. When my wife and I ride to the cinema, we squeeze both of our half-helmets into this bag and then hand carry the bag into the cinema.

When we go to the swapmeet or some other crowded event, I bring along my heavy duty locking cable which is intended to lock the motorcycle to a pole of some other handy, unmovable, item. We lace it through both helmets and occasionally, both jackets and may or may not loop it around a pole. However, after writing this, I have my security juices going again and that retractable Masterlock combination security cable is looking pretty good.

Stock Security

The fact that all motorcycles come with some sort of lock from the factory should tell you something about the possibility of motorcycle theft. Almost all have some sort of fork lock (unable to turn the front wheel) and ignition disables (no key, no run).

Fork Lock

This is either an internal lock with a fitted key or just a hole where you can place a padlock. The internal lock becomes lockable only when the front wheel is all the way to the left. Only with it in this extreme placement will you be able to lock it. The same goes for the padlock style. There are two metal plates, each with its own padlock hole and you cannot place the padlock through both holes until they are aligned one on top of the other. They only become aligned when the front wheel it turned all of the way to the left. When the front fork is locked, it will not allow you to move the front wheel. If somebody steals your bike, they will not be able to drive (or push) it anywhere but in a circle.

- I have heard that you can just jerk the handlebars hard and the built in lock will snap free. I tried that on my HD Wide Glide with no luck, it held strong. Maybe I am just not strong enough.
- HD provides a 'cam' key to make things more difficult for any lock pickers out there, (except those professionals who I used to dream about).
- Losing your key is bad but breaking it off in the lock is horrible.

Ignition Lock

Most bikes have this feature from the factory. You need a key to run the engine, that simple. No key, no ignition available. This is another line of defense against thieves. Can it be defeated, well probably it can. It is the same thing as "hot-wiring" a car. I doubt if it would be very quick and easy.

Physical Security

The factory provides a pretty good line of simple theft deterrent (fork lock and ignition disable) but don't forget about those four big guys who want to just lift your bike up and throw it in the back of their pickup.

So the next line of defense is to secure your bike to some unmovable object like a telephone pole or a sturdy fence pole. I know that I do not have to say what I am about to say but I'll say it anyway. Make sure your unmovable object is not something like a 4 inch galvanized pipe cemented into the ground but only 4 foot tall. Those four big guys would now be laughing like crazy as they lifted up you bike and threw it into the back of their pickup.

Chain and Lock

Buy a chain and a lock to secure your bike to the unmovable object. Here's where the compromises start to take place. Whatever chain you get, you need to keep it with you all the time so you have it when you want it. You will probably not want my 8 foot 2 inch monster wrapped around your sissy bar. It would be like riding 2-up all of the time. So you (like me compromise) and get a lighter chain or one of those steel cables coated with rubber and has a lock built in. Now you have at lease something that will keep the 'honest' people from stealing your bike. Be creative and find some unobtrusive place where you have wrap your chain around you bike when you are not using it.

Disc Brake Lock

Another option is the disc brake lock. It locks onto your disc and prevents the motorcycle from moving more than one revolution of the wheel while it is locked to the disc. Because, it is easy to forget about this lock when you get ready to go, most have a brightly colored chord that runs from the lock and clips onto the handlebars. If you forget that the lock is in place, you will see the chord when you sit down on your bike. The good news is that this lock is very effective and relatively small and light for transport. The bad news is that is does not lock your bike to an unmovable object. It is another line of defense thought and that may be what saves your bike.

If you try to think like a thief for a moment, you are considering stealing this bike and you would see the disc lock and just move on to a different target of opportunity. In this case, the disc lock has done its job, unless of course, the thief really wants your bike and not any other.

Alarms

There are numerous types of after market (add-on) motorcycle alarms with many different features to choose from. At the very bottom of the scale is a simple door intrusion alarm intended to hang on a doorknob (hotel room) and when moved, emits a loud shrieking alarm. This may be all you need for your specific application such as parking your bike in your garage and wanting to know when it is moved. Sometimes, the obvious solution really is the best solution. However, this simple solution will only work in a controlled environment like your garage. Out on the street, the only thing you can hope for is that the thief will get such a laugh out of seeing this hanging on your bike, they will take pity on your and move on to the next bike.

Basic Alarm

Next up comes the built in motorcycle alarm. Even the most basic alarm has a coupe of very good features. One, it does not go into your backpack or saddlebag when not in use like the hotel room door alarm. It becomes part of your bike and is always ready to go into action. And second, it usually has a blinking LED which may make all of the difference when you want the thief to move on to the next bike. These very basic alarms usually have a protected mercury switch (like in your house thermostat) which will activate the alarm when the bike is moved. Moving the bike moves the switch and the mercury sloshes inside of its glass tube and closes the alarm contacts and bingo, the alarm is activated. The alarm may trigger a siren (attached to your bike) or start honking your bikes horn and flashing your bikes turn signals. That is just what you can expect from a basic alarm.

Installation is simple with the manufacturer providing wiring diagrams and instructions. Screwdrivers, wire cutters/strippers and the like are about all you need. Some kits have specific harness plug-ins which are built specifically for your bike. It may take one to three hours to install it and you are ready.

Will it do the job for you? It all depends upon the environment and what your security (maybe budget) goals happen to be.

Tips

- Remember to conceal the alarm wiring. The thief may have installed a few motorcycle alarms themselves and will know just what to cut to disable the alarm. The more sophisticated alarms have a feature that activates the alarm whenever a critical wire is cut.

Advanced Alarm

Next up are the advanced features. Remote controls to activate the alarm system, negative switches to protect saddlebags, pagers that will tell you that something is going on with your bike (outside of the cinema right now), proximity detection sensors that will start the alarm chirping when someone simply gets too close to your bike, ignition disablers and just about anything else you want to build into your alarm system.

I bought one of these "Cadillac" systems and here's my experience. I bought an after market alarm from the same vendor who builds the Harley stock alarm. This was in 2006 and I think Harley has a different vendor now. It was modular so I could select each feature I wanted just like ordering a meal from a restaurant menu. I had to have the pager so I could put it on my nightstand and sleep at night. I had to have the proximity feature to keep the curious away from the bike. All in all, it cost around $400 and I installed it.

Installation was easy as it came with factory plug-ins (extra charge) so I did just about everything by simply removing the seat and plugging in the alarm. I did run a battery wire and had to place the pager antenna under my gas tank protector. It was a 45 minutes job, no sweat.

I had a remote/pager with a window (like a cell phone window) that showed me all kinds of alarm and battery status information. Activating the alarm brought an audible chirp from the bike which verified it was activated. Deactivating the alarm brought a couple of chirps which told me that the alarm was off. The pager has both vibrate and audible tones to tell me when the bike alarm was going off if I was inside and could not see the bike. The range to receive this info was pretty good, a few hundred feet. The range from the pager back to the bike was a lot less, maybe 75 feet.

If I walked up to the bike when the alarm was activated, at about three feet away, the bike would start chirping to warn me it was armed. The flashing LED was the built in Harley alarm light in the speedometer cluster. It worked great. After six months I took it off.

- Why? Well, the proximity sensor started chirping during the night whenever a cat would jump on the seat (The bike was parked outside in our apartment complex). Eventually, I disabled this feature.
- The alarm itself was rated at 400dB (I think) and it sounded loud when you were right next to the bike but from a half a block away, it wasn't even annoying. My point is that the alarm was not loud enough.
- Sometimes the alarm would trigger for no apparent reason sending me barefoot out into the parking lot in the middle of the night. I wonder what I would have done if I had actually confronted a thief in the middle of stealing my bike. T-shirt, Levis, barefoot, sleepy with my hair sticking out like Bozo the Clown, maybe I would have just scared him away with just my look.
- The Harley (2006 Wide Glide) came with a built in ignition disable and light flasher alarm. This was activated with a pretty cool little key fob. This system was in conflict with the after-market system I installed and I was never sure what alarm was on or off and I

always had to press my remote/pager plus the HD key fob.

But I could live with all of that. The straw that broke the camels alarm back, so to speak, was the morning that I got on the bike to go to work and the battery was dead. I got the bike going and stopped using my after market alarm. A few days later I removed the alarm and sent it back to the manufacturer complaining about all of the above and I received a polite e-mail and a replacement alarm in the mail. I was not interested in re-installing the alarm and chancing another dead battery. My $400 alarm is sitting on a shelf in my den destined for eventual "as-is" sale on E-Bay. Now I use the stock HD ignition disable and a chain. Who knows, maybe the alarm was not guilty of the dead battery?

But that does not mean that you will have the same experience. I say go for it and get what you want to suit your riding habits, your street environment, and your budget. There are a lot of very cool alarms available and these folks who make these alarms would not still be around if they did not make a quality product.

Bottom Line

Every obstacle you can present to a potential thief, improves the odds of keeping your bike. Like I said at the start of this chapter, it's all about who wants your motorcycle the most, you or the thief.

What Does It Cost?

Disc brake lock	$18
Basic Alarm	$75 - $100
Advanced Alarm	$150 and up

Resources

Motorcycle Superstore	No matter what style of motorcycle you ride, Motorcycle Superstore has the gear you need.	motorcycle-superstore.com
J&P Cycles	J&P Cycles® started as a family business 29 years ago.	jpcycles.com

Windshield

Introduction

A few years ago, I bought a Suzuki 1400 Intruder from a guy near Auburn California. I drove it home to Reno, 70 miles away over the Sierras. The Intruder had a full windshield on and I had an hour and a half to enjoy it.

The road is mostly freeway, so I was doing 70 to 75 mph all the way. Half helmet, Panavision glasses and a windshield, I felt like I was sitting in my living room. I was riding in a huge air pocket of relatively still air behind the full windshield. The wind noise was about 20% of what I was used to without a windshield. My hands felt like they were hanging out of a car window, I was tempted to do that flat palm airplane thing in the wind, angle up, angle down, whoo hoo.

When I arrived home, I stepped off my new (new to me anyway) motorcycle and I felt fresh as if I had just run down to the corner store. No after ride rushing noise in my ears, no tear tracks across my cheeks, no bug guts on my nose, I was literally amazed. I had no idea that a windshield should make that much of a change.

The next day I took it off and it has never been back on. Why? Well, it just did not look cool. That's right, I would trade all of that comfort for a cool look. This Intruder 1400 is a very cool looking v-twin (Harley knock-off) and the windshield was huge. It looked like I had ridden through a Plexiglas telephone booth, and the telephone booth had stuck on the front of the motorcycle. I just could not deal with it.

So, end of this chapter on windshields? No, one experience does not make a trend. I never forgot how pleasurable that ride through the Sierras had been and so I started my own personal quest for the windshield that did not look like a telephone booth. But let's start at the beginning.

Do You Need A Windshield?

If you are just riding around town or easy country cruises where you rarely get over 40 to 45 mph, a windshield is not an issue. I don't seem to go anywhere without getting on a freeway or high speed highway just to get to a place where I can take an easy cruise. Once you get up to 50 mph, a windshield starts to have an impact. A lot of riders just tough it out and a lot of riders want a windshield even at the lower speeds.

A windshield will make your ride more comfortable, more enjoyable and about the only downside is some wind buffering which has a minor impact on handling.

A windshield will keep that stinging rain from pelting you but presumably, you are wearing a riding jacket that already does that for you. It won't keep the rain off your face as the windshield should be lower than your nose anyway.

The biggest reason everybody doesn't have a windshield is the cool factor. Windshields just do not look cool on cruisers. OK, now that's my opinion and you have your opinion, it's a personal style issue.

Most riders have a very quick yes or no attitude about windshields but if you are on the fence I have listed out all of the considerations so you will know what you are looking for and what to avoid when you go windshield shopping.

Considerations

I have to tell you that I rarely ride more than 150 to 200 miles at a stretch. If I was heading out on a longer ride, I would be the first guy putting a windshield on my bike. To me, a long ride is the time to take advantage of everything that will improve the quality of the ride or the comfort of the rider.

Some bikes look funny without a windshield. Whenever I see a motorcycle cop on a bike without a windshield, I immediately think they must be making a movie, it just doesn't look real. All of the big road bikes have the "windshield" look and most of the street bikes look goofy with a windshield. That's my opinion.

There are some very cool windshields out there, if you are windshield compatible. Lots of sizes, tints, quick release attachments (for looking cool in a flash), vents, and nick-knack pouches are all available. Some come with sturdy chrome supports crisscrossing the weak spots, some are all polycarbonate, some are acrylic, some have clever "hidden" attachments and some attachments could do double duty as a brush guard on the front of a Hummer. How about that BMW with the push-button electric angle adjustment?

Tips

- Stick with the clear, tints as the dark shades are hard to see through at night.
- Always mount the windshield below eye level for vision (rain or shine).
- Quick release attachments are just as quickly released by thieves.
- The windshield pushes so much air that it hurts gas mileage.

- Your height when measuring for windshields is measured from your waist up.

Windshield Height

Looking through the windshield is not a good idea. Not only is there the normal collection of road dust, bug splats and whatnot obstructing your vision, but when it is raining, windshield vision becomes very difficult. Each one of those raindrops grabs any light source and obscures the road ahead. This is why the windshield shroud is below your line of sight. Some folks like it above their line of sight and then they extend their head up higher when they need to see over the windshield.

Most manufacturers recommend selecting a windshield that will place the top of the windshield below you nose and above your Adams apple or chin. While this may become a trial and error adjustment, some manufacturer web sites has sizing guides to help you.

Handling

Will adding a windshield affect the motorcycles handling ability? Sure, the bigger the windshield the bigger the chunk of air that is being pushed around the motorcycle. This is especially true in side winds. Remember that the size and the shape of the windshield is what will determine the amount of wind protection (and air resistance).

Is this a contract breaker? No, unless you are really dedicated to the highest possible performance, I don't think that adding a windshield will be a big deal.

Installation

There are numerous styles of windshield and numerous types of attachments. Your windshield manufacturer's installation instructions have the answers. Some windshields are attached to the triple tree, others to the handlebars. Some are easily adjustable and some are very static depending on the attachment to offer angle and height adjustments. Overall, it is very easy to install a windshield. Some subsequent adjustments may take some trial and error time. However you do it, you must remember that you are putting a big (or moderate) sail onto the bike and there can be tremendous wind pressures at work when you are riding at speed. Keep your cables free from contact with the windshield. It may look OK but remember, there is constant vibration and the potential for damage to your cables is real. The windshield must be secure, no Mickey Mouse duct tape installations.

The Search for a Windshield

It was not hard to narrow down the list of possible windshields. No farings, no full standards, and a "maybe" on both the handlebar mount. Before I go on though, I want to point out that since I finished evaluating windshields, I have seen some farings that look interesting. It really gets down to the style of motorcycle you either have or the look you want for your bike.

Faring

Originally designed to provide better aerodynamics, the faring does double duty by providing wind protection. How much or how little wind protection will be provided, is determined by the size and the shape of the faring. Typically, this is a sport bike item.

Handlebar Mount

This is a small, aerodynamic windshield. The nice feature of this type of windshield is that it is built (generally) to fit down and around the headlight. This has a big impact in preventing the under-windshield wind.

Full Standard

This is the big boy that comes to mind when you think of a motorcycle windshield. It does come in various sizes and from various manufacturers. Generally it is designed for your specific bike and your preferences in size and style.

WindVest

Figure 34 WindVest

Is a unique product that provides minimal wind protection. What is unique about the WindVest is that as it is made from very sturdy Plexiglas, it attaches to the motorcycle with a single low handlebar attachment. This eliminates the structural metal and other attachments seen on the larger windshields. It has a very clean look.

Bottom Line

Windshields seem to be one of those things that people love or hate. You can get a more comfortable ride at the cost of losing some of the cool look. Or maybe you need a windshield just to look cool.

That's it.

What Does It Cost?

Faring	$600
Handlebar Mount	$185
Full Standard	$250
WindVest	$300

Resources

Clearview Shields	Custom tailored windshields	clearviewshields.com
Memphis Shades	Full line of windshields and windscreens	memphisshades.com
National Cycle	(since 1937): Full line of windshields	nationalcycle.com
Rifle Farings	Cruiser Windshields and Farings	rifle.com
Slipstreamer	Full line of windshields	slipstreamer.com
WindVest	Handlebar mount specialty windshield/screens	WindVest.com

And of course, do not overlook your bikes manufacturer for products that were made specifically for your bike.

MISTAKES

This is the running summary of the top beginning rider mistakes.

Skipped the Basic MSF Rider Course

If you must make every mistake in the book please do not make this one. The MSF Basic Rider Course will reward you with the essentials you must have before you ever get out in the traffic on your motorcycle.

Don't Buy a Sportster

In the Harley family of motorcycles, the Sportster is the entry level ride. It comes in two main flavors, the 883 cc and the 1200cc. I bought the more powerful (read expensive) 1200 cc because I had heard some bikers call the 883 cc a girl's bike. Who cares what they say, the 883 looks like a 1200, is just as fast and is less expensive.

My heart wanted a chrome monster Softtail but my budget dictated a Sportster. Everyone told me that when you start with a Sportster after about 6 months you will want to upgrade to the big Harley. They were right.

If you are a new rider or a re-entry rider, we all make this mistake. Your first motorcycle should be a "starter" motorcycle. Get a used Japanese cruiser, 250 to 500 cc. It is light weight, easy to handle and cheap. Find out if riding a motorcycle is really what you want to do. If not sell it. If you are still jazzed after 3,000 miles, now you are experienced enough to make a more informed Harley purchase.

Lost Focus

You are not in a car. You cannot afford to go ten miles daydreaming about your sweetie, your job or anything else but the task at hand. Stay focused on riding. I cannot say enough about this. It can be a life and death mistake!

Wear the Proper Rider Gear

I know it's hot. I know it's just six blocks to the store. Never get on your motorcycle without the proper gear. The asphalt doesn't care if you have been riding five minutes or five hours, it's still awful damn hard and unforgiving.

Always Check Your Bike before You Ride

Check your tire pressure. Make a visual check. Do you have gas? Are your bungee tie downs secured? Stuff happens, things change and it is too tempting to just hop on and fire it up. Two minutes spent checking can save you hours with a tow truck or an ambulance ride.

Ran Out Of Gas

Check the gas gauge? Sure, but with experience will be checking both the gauge and the mileage. There always isn't a gas station around every bend. You know how many miles you have in your tank. Running out of gas is not only embarrassing and time consuming but on a motorcycle, it can be downright dangerous.

Out-riding Your Skill Level

New riders aren't even sure what their skill level is let alone when they are out-riding it. Statistically, out-riding your skill level is a leading cause of solo motorcycle crashes. If you don't know your skill level, find out and don't find out the hard way by out-riding it.

Understand "Go Where You Look"

Is this a phenomenon or a law of physics? I don't know and I don't care. I just know that it is 100% absolutely the truth, your motorcycle will go where you are looking. Look ahead at the apex of a curve and you will track right there. Look at that tree on the side of the road and oh well, "Hello" tree.

Ignored the Buffer Zone

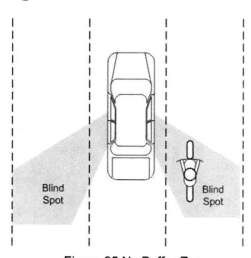

Figure 35 No Buffer Zone

They can't hit you if your not there! Stay away from cars. Don't be ridiculous about it, but even in heavy traffic, you can always maintain some buffer zone around you. Anticipate the soccer mom in the SUV, on a cell phone, changing lanes right into you. You know she is going to do it so keep your buffer zone and stay alive.

Didn't Understand Counter Steering

Want to go left? Push the left side of the handlebar. Go right? Push the right side of the handlebar. Hey, it's not a bicycle so don't try to ride it like a bicycle. Practice, practice and practice are the three things you must do to master this technique.

Put The Kickstand Down!

Whenever you hear about someone forgetting to put the kickstand down, it is always couched with the opening phrase, "I knew a guy who…" That's because forgetting to put the kickstand down is way beyond embarrassing. Have I ever forgotten to put the kickstand down? Not me, nope, not me. However I knew a guy… Yes, I forgot one time and only one time! And I am not the only one. There will never be an accurate statistic on how many riders forget to put the kickstand down as it is just too embarrassing. It's like getting personal information on someone's sex habits; in fact, it is probably easier to get someone's sex habit information than getting any motorcycle rider to admit to this goof-ball mistake.

CONCLUSION

"That's my story and I'm sticking to it."

If you think riding a motorcycle is for you, enroll in the MSF Basic Rider course and get started. If you have any doubts before you take the course, you will know for sure by the time you have finished the course.

If you like my advice, follow it. If you do not agree with what I have said, follow your own path. I don't know all of the answers but I have made a ton of mistakes. I have tried to outline these mistakes so you do not do the same.

Riding a motorcycle is more than just getting from point A to point B. It's a sport. It's a hobby. For some, it's a complete life style. Whatever it is to you, just have fun.

Index

I can be reached online at

www.WordCutter.com.

I am happy to receive your comments, and ideas. I cannot always answer each and every e-mail but I do read them all. I maintain a blog at the WordCutter website. Check it out for updates and resources.